PRINCIPLES OF STRUCTURAL TYPOLOGY

JANUA LINGUARUM

STUDIA MEMORIAE
NICOLAI VAN WIJK DEDICATA

edenda curat

C. H. VAN SCHOONEVELD

INDIANA UNIVERSITY

SERIES MINOR

NR. 62

1968

MOUTON

THE HAGUE · PARIS

PRINCIPLES
OF STRUCTURAL
TYPOLOGY

by

B. USPENSKY

1968

MOUTON

THE HAGUE · PARIS

LIBRARY OF CONGRESS CATALOG CARD NUMBER: 68-17893

Printed in the Netherlands by Mouton& Co., Printers, The Hague.

PREFACE TO THE ENGLISH TRANSLATION

This book was written in 1961 and first published in Russian in 1962 under the title *Principy strukturnoj tipologii* (Moscow University Press, 1962). It was conceived as a brief summary of certain ideas which were to be further elaborated in a more comprehensive exposition. It is therefore but natural that it should have been presented in the form of an introduction into the subject.*

This also accounts for the fact that some of the more recent publications have not been covered (in particular, the problems of language universals could only be touched upon; its more detailed discussion can be found in our book of 1965). The author is, of course, fully aware of certain shortcomings which are partly due to the conciseness of the book.

Moscow, July 28, 1967.   B. Uspensky

---

* The more comprehensive exposition of the theory was made later on in a much more voluminous monograph *Strukturnaja tipologija jazykov* [Structural Typology of Languages] (Moscow, "Nauka" Publishing House, 1965).

FOREWORD

The book consists of two parts.

The first, introductory part deals with the subject and the general aims of structural linguistic typology as well as the connections of typology with other trends of linguistic analysis. Some distinctive methodological features of structural typology are defined on the basis of a critical discussion of different typological trends in linguistics. The concept of *étalon language* (metalanguage) proposed as a standard for language comparison is also discussed there.

In the second, principal part the author attempts to set up an original typological theory based on a special system of terms and assumptions, in connection with which an investigation of the grammatical structure of the étalon language is undertaken. This structure is defined in terms of a specially developped interpretation of the traditional morphological classification of languages. The typological characteristics of a concrete language are defined in terms of transformations necessary for converting its structure to that of the étalon language. The book also discusses the possibility of building up special étalon languages for specific typological purposes with a view to attaining a more detailed typological characterization.

CONTENTS

I

THE OBJECT AND METHODS OF
STRUCTURAL TYPOLOGY

0. *The Subject and Aims of Structural Typology*

Typological methods of investigation have long been applied in linguistics. They have, however, in the course of the last ten years acquired ever greater importance. This is directly connected with the general quest for exact methods of linguistic investigation, in particular, for describing linguistic facts in terms of a calculus (i.e. of a system of formalized axioms and formal rules of deduction). This presupposes as a natural and necessary prerequisite the elimination of terminological confusion; this involves in its turn the definitions of the terms and assumptions used. It is natural to define the terms in such a way that they are independent of the specific character of a given language, and suitable for the description of any language.

The tendency to work out exact methods of linguistic research has been to a considerable extent brought to life by the practical problems modern linguistics has to face — machine translation, mechanical information retrieval, etc. In the realization of this tendency special importance is attached to the contemporary methods of investigation, in particular the methods of structural linguistics.

In the present book, therefore, is discussed the typological investigation of language in its contemporary stage, i.e. structural typology. As has been rightly observed by A. Kroeber, "comparisons today can have more meaning than they would have had before the phoneme and morpheme concepts were formulated".[1] Indeed, such methodological principles as differentiation of *langue*

---

[1] A. Kroeber, "On typological indices I: ranking of languages", *IJAL*, XXVI (1960), 3.

and *parole* (F. de Saussure), differentiation of *emic* and *etic* levels in language (i.e. the distinction between such phenomena as phonemes, morphemes, graphemes on the one hand and their variants on the other — as proposed by K. Pike[2]), the examination of language phenomena on the *plan d'expression* and the *plan du contenu* (L. Hjelmslev and his school) enables us to distinguish the essential from the accidental in the phenomena of language, and thus to reveal its structure. Such methods, as distributional analysis, transformational analysis, etc., make it possible to do this in a comparatively exact way. Indeed, it seems fully warranted to take the structure of a language as a starting point in typological linguistic comparison — otherwise one compares isolated phenomena which *per se* (apart from their relations with other phenomena in the respective language) may not be informative. If the various structures are described in adequate terms and based upon identical assumptions (later we shall try to show that some assumptions are indispensable in a sufficiently exhaustive linguistic description), then the comparison of these structures is the subject of structural typology. Thus, structural typology can be understood as a systematization, a cataloguing, an inventarization, an arrangement of linguistic phenomena from different languages according to their specific structural features (i.e. features, essential from the point of view of the structure of each given language).

The main problems of typology follow from its definition.

As a result of typological investigations we may speak of some features that exist in all languages or such features that, on the contrary, cannot be found in any language whatsoever; we can connect separate phenomena with each other and from one phenomenon predict another, i.e. establish typological laws. Thus we can speak of the distinctive features of language, in contrast with, for instance, other semiotic systems. Hence, one of the fundamental tasks of typology is the construction of a general theory of language, the establishing of the correlations and characteristics pertaining to any language, i.e. language universals.

[2] *See* K. L. Pike, *Language in Relation to a Unified Theory of the Structure of Human Behaviour*, Part. I *Prelim* (Glendale, 1954).

Let us give some examples of such correlations from different linguistic levels. In all languages syllables exist that begin with a consonant, and that end with a vowel; there are no languages without stop consonants; if in a language the contrast stop — affricate exists, for instance [t] — [ts], then there is also the fricative [s];[3] there is a complex interrelation between the contrast in a language between short and long vowels and dynamic stress. In respect to other levels we may point out the established interrelation between gender (contrast between active and passive classes of nouns) and number;[4] between aspect and tense;[5] between the position of the adjective and the position of the adverb in a language;[6] between the case of nouns and agreement of the verb in a language;[7] and we may also point out the dependence of the fixedness of word-order on the distinctness of the formal characteristics of words in a language.[8] The examples given do not exhaust the results obtained in this field.

And so the first object of typology is to reveal the isomorphous phenomena, common to all languages. At the same time, typology deals with specific features characteristic of certain languages. On this basis it is possible to classify languages. The investigation of linguistic universals and the classification of languages on the basis of structural features (typological classification) are directly connected with each other — the one implying the other. Indeed, the object of typological classification is to create a maximally econom-

[3] See R. Jakobson, "Typological studies and their contribution to historical comparative linguistics", Proceedings of the 8-th International Congress of Linguists (Oslo, 1958).
[4] See V. V. Ivanov, "Tipologija i sravnitel'no-istoričeskoe jazykoznanie" [Typology and comparative-historical linguistics], Voprosy jazykoznanija, 1958, 5, p. 36.
[5] See J. Kuryłowicz, L'apophonie en indo-europeen (Wroclaw, 1956), pp. 24-35; idem "Aspect en temps dans l'histoire du Persan", Rocznik orientalisticzny, XVI, (1953).
[6] J. H. Greenberg, "The Nature and Uses of Linguistic Typologies", IJAL, XXIII (1957), 2.
[7] B. A. Uspensky, "Opyt transformacionnogo issledovanija sintaksičeskoj tipologii" [An attempt to transformational investigation of syntactical typology], Issledovanija po strukturnoj tipologii, Moscow, 1963.
[8] E. Sapir, Jazyk [Language] (Moscow-Leningrad, Socekgiz, 1934), p. 50.

ical way of codifying the information about the structure of the languages of the world. Here, different languages are described by means of the same set of symbols. Thus, the isomorphism of various languages is revealed. The classification of languages on the basis of typology is intended to aid the investigation of unknown languages. The investigator, having discovered some regularities, is entitled to seek (or to assume hypothetically) features connected with these. The second object of typology (the classification of languages) is therefore closely linked with the first.

These are the fundamental tasks of typology: to discover isomorphism and allomorphism of various languages. Typology is an approach to the problem which has occupied linguistics of all times (from G. Leibnitz and the grammarians of the Abbey Port-Royal up to the Copenhagen structuralists) — the problem of a universal grammar. On the basis typology we can build up a system, common to all languages; by introducing complementary rules, subsystems are established, corresponding to specific languages. That is the way in which the two objects of typology are connected.

"... il n'est pas faux de prétendre ... qu'il n'existe qu'un langage humain, identique en son fond, sous toutes les lattitudes", as J. Vendryes wrote. — "C'est bien l'idée qui se manifeste dans les tentatives de linguistique générale".[9]

1.   Typology in Relation to Some Other Trends of Linguistic Research

Let us examine the relation between typology and some other trends of linguistic investigation.

First, the relation between the typology and the comparative philology. Here, we must take into account the fact that in many respects the typological methods are contrasted with the comparative ones; the interest of many linguists in typology is connected

---

[9]   J. Vendryes, *Le langage. Introduction linguistique à l'histoire* (Paris, 1921), p. 274.

with criticism of the comparative method (N. Trubetzkoy[10]). These methods are therefore often opposed to each other. This explains why typology (at least at its contemporary stage) makes relatively little use of the achievements of comparative linguistics. However, a "diachronic typology", i.e. an effective comparison of structures representing synchronic sections of a language in various stages of its development, is certainly justified.

One can determine e.g. which changes (phonetic, grammatical, etc.) and under what structural conditions, are possible in the diachronic development of a language, and which are not. One can determine and investigate the panchronic structural patterns which remain invariant in the diachronic transformations of languages. E. Sapir found, for example, that the phonetic pattern (the system of mutually opposed sounds in language) is preserved longer than the quality of these sounds, i.e. the sounds change but their oppositions with other sounds remain.[11] These are obviously not the only cases where the results of the comparative method can be used for typological purposes.

At the same time, the typological method is found to be helpful to comparative-historical linguistics and supplements it in many respects.[12] Indeed, the traditional comparative analysis, as is well known, does not reconstruct the system of a language, but gives a mere collection of forms without indication of their interrelation. In all probability, the reconstructed proto-forms belong to different synchronic stages (which was not realized by A. Schleicher when he wrote a fable in the indoeuropean proto-language). At the same time the typological methods allow us to work on the synchronic system of the proto-language, enabling us to deduce certain facts

[10] *See* N. S. Trubetzkoy, "Mysli ob indoevropejskoj probleme" [Conceptions of the Indoeuropean problem], *Voprosy jazykoznanija*, 1958, 1. In this work genetic problems are solved with typological methods; six structural features are given to which the concept "indoeuropean" can be reduced.
[11] *See* E. Sapir, "Sound Patterns in Language", *Selected writings of Edward Sapir*, (Berkley and Los-Angelos, 1949), pp. 33-45.
[12] On the necessity of applying the typological method in comparative-historical investigation see J. Vendryes, "La comparaison en linguistique", *Bulletin de la société de linguistique de Paris*, XLI (1946), fasc. 1, no. 124 (Paris, 1946), pp. 5-6.

from other ones which are related to them. Once we know the correlation of phenomena (typological rules) it is possible to predict one phenomenon from another. For instance: if in a language labialized front vowels are found, we must assume the existence of labialized back vowels; the findings of typology challenge the existence in the Proto-Indoeuropean of voiced aspirate consonants on the basis of the fact that no actual language exhibits such a system of oppositions as is reconstructed for the proto-language.[13] Indeed, if we know the rules which govern language in general, we may conclude as to what is possible and what is not possible in a particular language, and on these grounds select the facts, comparing them to others. Typological studies make it possible to predict certain structural features of a reconstructed language and determine the typological probability of a certain reconstruction as well. For instance, we succeed in reconstructing the Proto-Indoeuropean with only one vowel; but we must prove beforehand that such a phenomenon is typologically possible. The existence of languages with one vowel phoneme (Aranta, Abaza) has been proved possible from concrete language material.[14] This provides the typological basis on which to develop analogously the reconstruction of the proto-language.

Thus, the typological methods greatly contribute to comparative-historical linguistics. The structural-typological and comparative methods are contrasted in as far as synchrony and diachrony can in general be opposed in language. Indeed, structural typology is primarily connected with the synchronic description of language, while the comparative method with the diachronic one. In so far as we can envisage the development of a language in time as a succession of synchronic cross-sections, we can speak of the employment of typological methods in comparative-historical linguistics.

It may furthermore be pointed out that particular typological

[13]   See R. Jakobson, op. cit.
[14]   See S. D. Kacnel'son, "K fonologičeskoj interpretacii protoindoevropejskoj zvukovoj sistemy [On the phonological interpretation of the proto-indeuropean sound system], Voprosy jazykoznanija, 1958, 3. W. S. Allen, "Structure and system in the Abaza verbal complex", Transactions of the Philological society (Hertford, 1956).

methods have long been applied in comparative-historical linguistics. In particular, typology of groups of cognate languages has always been used: if in all (the majority) of the languages of a given group a certain category exists, it is ascribed to the respective proto-language. In this sense, the proto-language represents the totality of information on the typology of the given group of languages.[15]

We may note that in a definite sense comparative-historical linguistics can be treated as a particular kind of typological comparison, *viz.* a typology of correspondences between *plan d'expression* and *plan du contenu* (on the material of different languages). If we would single out (together with Sapir, Greenberg and some other scholars) a special symbolic linguistic level (i.e. a level which deals with relations between form and content, while all the other levels deal with form without content or with content without form), then we might think of a symbolic typology — side by side with a grammatical typology, a phonological one, etc. In this sense we may speak both of symbolic universals (the presence of a nasal in the word denoting the female parent may illustrate the point) and of typological classification on the symbolic level (i.e. comparative historical linguistics).

Let us examine the correlation between the typological and descriptive linguistics.

The typological study of a language — i.e. the investigation of a language as compared with all other languages — contrasts with the tendency of some investigators to describe a language exclusively by the means provided by the given language (i.e. without applying to any other language). This is especially characteristic of the descriptivists, who sometimes made this tendency into a methodological principle.

This contrast has long been felt. C. Voegelin refers to the conflict between "the ideology of Boas" (the tendency to describe every language proceeding from its specific "spirit") and "the Boas plan of language description" (suggesting a universal scheme for all

---

[15] *Cf.* D. H. Hymes, "Positional analysis of categories", *Word*, XI (1955), 1.

languages).[16] This conflict is also characteristic of the glosse-
maticians. On the one hand, they try to propose certain absolute
methods, to make assertions that are true for any language, while
on the other — they tend to describe a language in the simplest
possible way: the choice of methods may depend on the purposes
of the description, on the material described, i.e. it may turn out
to be useful to apply different methods of description for different
languages.[17]

Each method has its advantages and supplements the other.
The correlation between the typological and the descriptive method
in synchronic linguistics is analogous with the correlation between
the comparative method and the method of internal reconstruction
in diachronic linguistics. According to R.Jakobson: "a description
of systems without their taxonomy, as well as a taxonomy without
description of single systems, is a flat contradiction in terms;
either one implies the other".[18]

It is remarkable that both the above mentioned tendencies have
alternated in the historical development of linguistics.

2. *Methods of Typological Investigation*

Various scholars have approached typological problems from
different angles. It is possible to propose a series of binary distinctive features, on the basis of which we may characterize the
method and trend of every investigation.[19] At the same time,

[16] C. F. Voegelin, "The Boas Plan for the Presentation of American Indian
Languages", *Proceedings of the American Philosophical Society*, 96, 1952,
pp. 439-451.
[17] *See* H. J. Uldall, *Outline of glossematics*, *TCLC*, X_1 1957, p. 23; E. Fischer-
Jørgensen, "On the definition of phoneme categories", *Acta Linguistica*, 1952,
VII, p. 11.
[18] R. Jakobson, *op. cit.*, p. 18.
[19] Thus a typological classification of typological investigations is made. Cf.
the attempt to classify typology by J. H. Greenberg (J. H. Greenberg, "The
Nature and Uses of Linguistic Typologies", *IJAL*, XXIII (1957), 2), by
V. Skalička (V. Skalička, "O současném stavu typologie", *Slovo a slovesnost*,
1958), 19.

a critical examination of the possible solutions will allow us to specify the method of structural typology.

The following grounds of subdivision (distinctive features) are proposed to characterize typological approaches:

2.1. *What is Subjected to Typological Comparison — Texts or Systems?*

The descriptivists treat language empirically as closed corpus of texts. Correspondingly typological characteristics from this point of view may ground on the direct comparison of the texts from various languages (and not their systems). As a result the relevance of information on the typology of the languages compared is fully conditioned by the nature of the texts selected for the typological comparison. The morphological classification of Greenberg[20] may serve as an example (Greenberg himself calls it "pragmatic").

In essence, the contrast "system — text" is identical with the contrast "language — speech" (*langue — parole*).[21] Structural typology should (by definition) proceed from systematic comparison; the analysis of text (*la parole*) should be combined with the modeling of the system of the language (*la langue*), i.e. of a certain internal system, which lies at the basis of every act of speech. (In terms of logic, *langue* is the meta-*parole*, i.e. a certain system against the background of which the phenomena of *parole* themselves become systematic[22]).

At the same time the investigator, analysing a language, always works with a concrete text; if he seeks to model the system of a language, he has to hypothesize the relevance or non-relevance of certain phenomena, observed in the text under investigation (i.e.

[20] J. H. Greenberg, "A quantitative approach to the morphological typology of language", *IJAL*, XXVI (1960), 3.

[21] The dilemma — text and system, *langue* and *parole* — also exists in the methodology of mathematical linguistics, where the investigators choose between analysis and synthesis (modeling) of language.

[22] The meaning of the prefix *meta-* is defined later.

that certain phenomena, observed in the text, are characteristic for that language or, on the contrary, are accidental in this text) and he has to carry out a preliminary analysis of the text (modeling the system and excluding the extra-systematic phenomena from examination).

Thus, structural analysis involves the process of hypothesizing and is connected with a preliminary analysis of text.[23]

2.2. *What is Subjected to Typological Comparison — All Languages or Separate Languages (Groups of Languages)?*

In other words, the question can be put thus: does induction take place? Typological investigations proceed, as a rule, from a limited number of languages, but they inductively assign certain features to all languages; later we shall test at random how far this induction is justified. Thus, certain inductively established general typological regularities lie at the basis of the comparison. They are considered irrespectively of the number of languages which are to be compared; it is assumed that any $n+1$ language will fit in this given scheme. (In deductive typological constructions the inductive analysis determines the initial system of terms and assumptions.)

A group of linguists (led by V. Mathesius) do not accept such an induction, opposing "characterology" with typology.[24] Proceeding from the material of a given group of languages, they confine themselves to its characteristics. The already mentioned structural features which were suggested by N. Trubetzkoy (typologically defining the Indoeuropean group of languages) may serve as an example; E. Benveniste pointed out that these six features may not be regarded as a definition of the concept "Indoeuropean", demonstrating this in a purely typological way: he found an

---

[23]   Cf. H. Spang-Hanssen, *Probability and structural classification in language description* (Copenhagen, 1959).
[24]   See V. Mathesius, "On linguistic Characterology with Illustrations from Modern English", *Actes du Ier Congrès internationale de linguistes* (Leiden, 1928).

obviously non-Indoeuropean language (the language Takelma, Oregon) for which all six features hold.[25]

E. Benveniste considers it impossible to define historical concepts in typological terms;[26] apparently this statement can be applied to all extra-linguistic concepts.

2.3. What is Subjected to Typological Comparison — Language as a Whole or Languages Within the Scope of Some Level?

Some linguists worked on the complex characterization of languages or language groups (cf. the "characterology" of V. Mathesius and the typological definition of genetic groups by N. Trubetzkoy). However, with a complex comparison of the various languages we may apparently find any number of distinctive features and, at the same time, the features may not exclude each other.

For the systematization of these features it is expedient to carry out typological comparison independently on different linguistic levels: phonological, grammatical, etc. It should be noted in this connection that the differentiation of a morphological and a syntactic levels does not appear to be always typologically justified, as the borderline between these levels is itself a characteristic of a language. The object of a "morphological classification" thus becomes indefinite.

At the present stage of research a consistent comparison of languages as wholes is hardly feasible; in most cases the efforts of contemporary scholars are directed towards a comparison of language structures within the scope of one level, for instance, of the level of phonology, morphology, syntax (or the grammar as a whole), vocabulary, etc. However, such a comparison is possible

[25] E. Benveniste, "La classification des langues", *Conferences de l'Institut de linguistique de l'Université de Paris*, XI, 1954, pp. 41-42. We should note that N. Trubetzkoy himself did not consider the presence of his six features sufficient to define a language as Indoeuropean; he still speaks about an undetermined criterion of a sufficient number of lexical correspondences (N. S. Trubetzkoy, *op. cit.*, p. 70.
[26] *Idem*, pp. 42-43.

in principle. It will turn out to be very rewarding, if one verifies and proves the hypothesis of the balance between the simplicity of some and the complexity of other parts of the language system (vowels: consonants; declension: conjugation; grammatical structure: vocabulary, etc.). This was conjectured by linguists such as A. Meillet, V. Brøndal, L. Ščerba, N. Jakovlev. More recently the hypothesis of a relationship between the different levels of a language has been proposed by R. Jakobson. The verification of these hypotheses, however, presupposes the elaboration of the methods of structural typology.

2.4. *What is the Basis of Typological Characterization: Types or Features?*

In other words: is a language characterized on the ground of its specific features or by means of correlating it directly with a certain language type?

Schlegel, Humboldt, Steinthal, Misteli and Finck classify languages according to their correspondances with definite language types (without explicit definition of features determining this or that type). The greater part of languages, however, does not fit within this scope: one can only speak of the degree of correspondence between a given language and a given type. Thus, we do not achieve a distinct division: one and the same language may be to some degree agglutinative, to some degree inflected, etc. It seems appropriate, however, to proceed not from the types but from primary distinctive features; on this basis it is possible to carry out the characterization of different languages (E. Sapir, J. H. Greenberg) as well as the characterization of different language types (V. Skalička[27]).

The merit of E. Sapir is that he introduced coordinates into the classification of languages, characterizing languages directly by a set of complementary features. Evidently, the more features there are, the more detailed the language classification will be.

[27] *See* his books: *Typ češtiny*, (Prague, 1951); *Zur ungarischen Grammatik*, (Prague, 1935).

Such "coordinate" comparison of languages appears absolutely necessary, for language is not uni-dimensional: for its description we need at least two dimensions (cf. syntagmatic and paradigmatic axes).

Therefore, when we characterize languages in terms of one single characteristics (i.e. in one dimension), we characterize uni-dimensional constructions instead of languages. J. H. Greenberg has remarked, that typological classifications usually do not define languages but rather definite constructions that are characteristic of a language.[28] Then it becomes necessary to determine to what extent a given construction is characteristic (representative) of the language under investigation (this can be done statistically). The typological characterization of a language (not a construction) can be achieved by the introduction of certain supplementary bases of comparison, i.e. by the introduction of coordinates.

2.5. *Is Information about a Language Based on Verbal or Quantitative Data, i.e. given in the form of quantitative indices?*

One can determine the typological specificity of a language by posing some questions on its structure. The answers to these questions may be of two kinds: *yes — no* or in numerical indices. Quantitatively we can determine the degree of participation of a certain feature in the structure of a language, as well as the degree of correspondence of the analyzed language with a certain language type. We may express this degree in general terms (see the classification of E Sapir) or by numbers (cf. the classification of J. H. Greenberg).

It should be borne in mind, however, that any statistics presupposes a preliminary deterministic theory (before quantification we must define what is to be quantified). At the same time, statistics (in implicit or explicit form) is hard to avoid.

[28] J. H. Greenberg, "A quantitative approach to the morphological typology of language", *IJAL*, XXVI (1960), 3, p. 182.

Apparently we can accept the thesis that "the description of the system of a language (code) as such, may be given by methods of mathematical logic and set-theory without the aid of probabilities. But a probability analysis appears to be indispensable for the examination of a text (information) in its relation to the system (code)".[29]

This thesis enables us to develop a structural typology by non-quantitative methods.

Certain requirements to a typological theory are imperative for any typological investigation, irrespective of the direction and the methods of approach.

Thus a most accurate specification of the system of terms and assumptions is absolutely indispensable for any typological investigation.

As has been said, all typology primarily proceeds from a certain induction: some peculiarities belonging to a series of languages are inductively ascribed to over all languages. During this process, terms which are relatively clear in the case of the individual languages, lose their definite character. As a result the very idea of typological structuring becomes useless. Thus, the vagueness of terminology is the fundamental weakness of the majority of morphological classifications. It has already been mentioned that the very borders of "morphology" are defined by the typological specificity of the languages under examination. In the traditional morphological classification such concepts as "word", "preposition" ("postposition"), "affix" (the difference between the last two is not always clear), "incorporation", remain undefined.

Before developing a typology, one should define the terms. It is impossible to do this without certain assumptions. Absence of assumptions will inevitably lead to a vicious circle, since in that case

---

[29]   V. V. Ivanov, "Jazykoznanie i matematika" [Linguistics and mathematics], *Bjulleten' ob"edinenija po problemam mašinnogo perevoda*, 1957, 5, p. 8. Cf. H. Spang-Hanssen, *Probability and structural classification in language description* (Copenhagen, 1959), pp. 87-89. It is demonstrated in the last work, that the structure of a language can always be built up from empirically-obtained quantitative data in the form of qualitative indices.

terms would define themselves by themselves. An explicit formulation of the assumptions, which exist in any structural linguistic investigation [thus, we assume, that we know the language in question (i.e. that certain phenomena, observed in a concrete text, will be found in any text of that language); we also assume during the analysis of one linguistic level that somehow the problems of the other levels are solved, etc.], is especially important when studying typology.

Explicit definitions of terms and assumptions in use thus becomes a major precondition of typological studies.

When developing a typology it is necessary to choose an initial unit of correlation, serving as a point of departure in the comparison of different languages (and the primary point of typological linguistic analysis). This unit should be defined in such a manner that its existence in every language appears self-evident. On the grammatical level the initial unit of correlation may be represented by a morpheme, a word, a syntagma, etc. Typologies which are based on different initial units of correlation — seeing that adequate linguistic methods are applied — are complementary with respect to one another.

Another essential requirement in typological structuring is that of consistency, i.e. a maximum delimitation of the criteria of classification. The classification made by E. Sapir is significant in this respect.

It is obvious that the construction of a typology is connected with the preliminary solution of many questions; these questions concern the general understanding of the problems and objects of typology as well as the concrete problems of linguistic analysis. The fact that a different terminology can be used, and a different analysis can be made causes many difficulties in typological structuring.

There exists an ingenious attempt to use these very difficulties for the construction of a typological classification (C. E. Bazell[30]). Bazell proposes to change from the arguments to the objects of the arguments. Analyzing the linguistic controversies in various lan-

---

[30] C. E. Bazell, *Linguistic Typology* (London, 1958); *see* L. Zgusta's review in *Archiv Orientální*, XXVIII (1960), 4, pp. 682-684.

guages, he comes to the conclusion that different phenomena in different languages are subject to disagreement. Hence, we may classify linguistic phenomena on the basis of the specific problems they create in a uniform linguistic analysis, and correspondingly classify languages on the basis of this classification of phenomena.

The problematical character of the following factors in particular is examined:

(1) The possibility of unambiguous segmentation (whether drawing a line between grammatical elements in a syntagmatic sequence can be performed in different ways).

(2) The possibility of a unambiguous classification (whether paradigmatic subdivision of grammatical elements, i.e. uniting them in classes, can be performed in different ways).

Three types of languages can be distinguished on the basis of the answer to these problems:

(1) The classification of languages does not cause controversy, but their segmentation gives rise to disagreement (e.g. Latin).

(2) Drawing a line between the elements does not cause difficulties, but their classification gives rise to disagreement (Chinese, Vietnamese).

(3) The classification and segmentation of the elements are possible to the same degree (e.g. Turkish).

We can see, that, according to the results, this classification of languages coincides with the classification made by A. Schlegel (inflected, agglutinative and amorphous languages), and can be regarded as one of its possible contemporary interpretations. The classification made by C. E. Bazell does not examine languages directly, but rather the attitude of linguists towards the languages (the author himself defines his typology as "problem typology"). In other words, it is not the structures of the languages that forms the immediate object of C. Bazell's typology, but the degree of simplicity (ambiguousness) with which these structures can be deduced (from the text). Consequently, C. Bazell's typology — though in itself necessary and interesting — is not a "structural typology" in the proper sense of the word (if we understand, as proposed above, "structural typology" as a typology of structures).

3. *Typology and Étalon-Language*

It can be seen from what has been expounded above that typological investigations are greatly hampered by lack of coordination of research, as well as by the absence of a generalized approach to the description of the typological inventory. Hence the lack of correspondence in the terminology, and in the principles of description of the various lingual phenomena.

A concrete criterion for the typological valuation is necessary.

The idea of invariance forms the basis of all linguistic comparisons (as well as of every comparison in general). We require an *étalon language* from which to proceed when typologically describing various languages. The étalon language is generally understood as an abstract language model which is used as a standard in typological comparison. On determining an étalon language and the rules of transformation from an étalon language to concrete languages under examination, it is possible to obtain a consistent and uniform description of these languages. An étalon language can thus be regarded as a metalanguage in relation to the described languages (in what follows the terms "metalanguage"[31] and "étalon-language" are used as synonyms). With respect to a definite grammatical level, e.g. the grammatical one, we can say that the characteristics of a certain language type (say, agglutinative) appear as the characteristics of metalanguage in relation to some other type of language (e.g., inflected) on condition that any language of the latter type can be described through a corresponding language of the former type (either natural or artificial).

The typological classifications were usually more or less intuitively oriented toward a certain hypothetical norm, i.e. a certain impicitely assumed language. This language, however, was not overtly postulated. This accounts to a great extent for the inefficiencies of these classifications. The employment of a metalanguage is

---

[31] The term "metalanguage" is adopted in linguistics apparently from logic (the works of R. Carnap). The prefix *meta-* is used for the designation of a language or theory, in the symbols of which another language or theory is described. In this way *metalanguage* is opposed to *object-language*.

indispensable in comparative analysis, it has always been used, though implicitly and vaguely. Its explicit determination should contribute to the success of the analysis.[32]

Generally speaking, any language can be used as a metalanguage. This happens actually in foreign language textbooks when, in characterizing the foreign language, the student's mother tongue is taken as an *étalon*; in describing dialects, when the dialects are regarded as deviations from the literary language; often in the description of unknown languages, when the language of the investigator serves as an *étalon* (but if the investigator knows several languages of different systems, the étalon language he uses will be modified). The first Latin grammars were described according to the Greek standard (e.g. Priscianus's grammar). Subsequently, however, a Latin-Greek metalanguage was used in compiling grammars of other European languages (e.g. Church Slavonic, English). Descriptions of national languages are often compiled in the same way.

Although this is not the best way of describing languages, it is nevertheless sufficiently consistent.

Sometimes a metalanguage is specially constructed — i.e. a certain system of symbols is set up, so that it is appropriate for the description of the object from some or other point of view.

Here, the most divergent levels and aspects of the language can be the object description. Thus, the distinctive features posited by R. Jakobson can be regarded as a metalanguage for phonology, the semantic fields and semantic factors, as a metalanguage for the vocabulary. The mediator language is the metalanguage of translation. Field workers also use a definite metalanguage when they compile questionnaires for their informant. In the sphere of diachronical linguistics the proto-language is to an increasing extent regarded as the metalanguage, whose historical authenticity thus becomes irrelevant.[33]

[32] The *parts of sentence* may be regarded as the result of the use in linguistics of the metalanguage of the Aristotelian logic (which, in its turn, one may apparently regard as the product of a certain linguistic analysis).
[33] *See* W. S. Allen, "Relationship in comparative linguistics", *Transactions of the Philological Society* (Hertford, 1953); V. V. Ivanov, "Teorija otnošenija

A structural typology can be set up by establishing a certain étalon language and transformations from the étalon language to concrete languages and vice versa (on different linguistic levels).

In the second part of this book a similar task for the grammatical level is undertaken. The structure of the étalon language is determined in terms of a specially elaborated interpretation of the traditional morphological classification of languages; languages are distinguished by the degree of their affinity with the étalon language — i.e. by the number of transformations from the given language to the étalon-language (the required transformations are indicated). We shall try to show the structural correlation between different types of languages by means of intralingual operations.[34]

The possibility to build a special (supplementary) étalon language for the solution of another (narrower) typological problem — the comparison of parts of speech in various languages — will also be demonstrated. On the basis of the latter it will become possible to compare languages complexly (i.e. to determine the degree of affinity between each of them and the étalon language) by means of several features at a time.

---

meždu jazykovymi sistemami i osnovanija sravnitel'no-istoričeskogo jazykoznanija" [A theory of the relation between language systems and the basis of comparative-historical linguistics], *Tezisy soveščanija po matematičeskoj lingvistike* (Leningrad, 1959), pp. 7-8.

[34] In doing this we shall as far as possible rely on the principle of the reversibility of the operations performed — i.e. on the possibility to revert to the initial state when performing a certain transformation.

A TENTATIVE THEORY OF STRUCTURAL
TYPOLOGY ON THE GRAMMATICAL LEVEL

0. *System of Terms and Assumptions*[1]

We assume that we possess certain information on each of the languages to be compared; this information can be described by introducing the following concepts.

0.1. *Grammaticalness* — It is assumed that once we know a language, we can always state whether a given sentence is grammatical or non-grammatical (cf. the experiment of L. V. Ščerba with "glokaja kuzdra" for the Russian language; analogous phrases were suggested by R. Carnap for German and Ch. Fries for English); all semantic anomalies being disregarded thus providing the possibility of an absolute substitution.

In fact, we may regard a language system as an infinite set of all possible combinations from a given number of elements, on which certain restricting rules are imposed. We can distinguish strata of semantic, stylistic, grammatic and other restrictions. Then, in

---

[1] We shall use the following symbols to formalize the notation: → "changes into ..." (the sign of one-sided transformation), ←→ "equivalent" (the sign of equivalence); root classes and word classes are designated by capital letters: *X* — class of roots, *N* — class of nouns, *A* — class of adjectives, *V* — class of verbs, *Adv* — class of adverbs; formative elements are registered in their concrete form (*a-*, *the*, *bi-*, *v*, etc.) or by small letters to designate their class (*n*, *m* — a certain class of formative elements).

The notation is linear — for instance, fusion and umlaut are represented as a sequence of components [an Arabic word is represented as a root + vocalism (+ change of the rootpattern if necessary)]; a reduplicated form is represented as a root + formative element, designating repetition (as is actually done in the Indonesian orthography). The whole process is performed on the emic level — i.e. a distributional analysis is supposed to be carried out, the identification of variants is performed, words of an anomalous structure are substituted by their structurally normal equivalents, elliptical constructions are completed.

order to investigate the grammatical structure of a language it is natural to disregard all restrictions other than the grammatical ones.

0.2.   *The element* — We can break up a sentence of any language into elements. By an element we mean the minimum productive morpheme or the fixed combination of morphemes possessing minimality and productivity.

Minimum, i.e. undivisible into productive morphemes.

Productive, i.e. having the ability to enter into various structural combinations. If the combinability of a certain morpheme cannot be indicated by listing concrete morphemes which form its environ-ment,[2] it may be called productive (English morphemes *good*, *-ly* can be adduced as examples). If there are two elements, such that one forms part of the other (for instance, *plenty* and *plentiful*), then the remainder, obtained as the result of subtraction (*-ful*) is a non-productive morpheme.[3]

The element is considered as the initial unit of correlation between languages. Sentences in different languages can be represented as strings of elements.

0.2.1.   Among the elements we can single out the formative ones. Then the elements of the various languages are divided into two groups:

group I — *root elements:* they cannot be presented as an ex-haustive list for a language.

group II — *formative elements:* they can be presented as an ex-haustive list from the outset. According to their interchangeability in a grammatical sentence they can be divided in a language into classes including the zero element as a possible member of a class) — in that case we shall say that they represent certain *cate-gories;* the elements, which do not form a class (i.e. such elements, that cannot be changed into others or omitted from their environ-

[2] The combinability of a productive morpheme is defined not in terms of concrete units of the language but in terms of certain classes — be it the class of root elements, a class of formative elements (*see* 0.2.1.) or a class of words (*see* 0.5.1).

[3] This is proved *a contrario*.

ment) — will be called *empty*. Some examples of formative elements of different kinds: the inflexion -*a* in the Russian *stol-a*, the vocalism and root pattern in the Arabic *yaktubu*, the element of reduplication in the Indonesian *orang-orang*, etc.

Thus, the formative elements are marked in a language. The difference between root elements and formative elements can be reduced to descriptive strategy: the description of a language consists of a dictionary and a grammar (the latter explaining how to form a sentence from the elements listed in the dictionary). In the case of an economic description, only the root elements will be listed in the dictionary, while the formative elements are most effectively assigned to the grammar.

0.2.1.1. Formative elements can be divided into obligatory and facultative elements. *Facultative* are those formative elements, that may in all cases be omitted from the sentence without disturbing its grammaticalness. For instance, the elements expressing gender and emphasis in English; deminutivity in Russian; number in Japanese and Indonesian; all categories in amorphous languages; the case (directive and object) in Hebrew; conation, intensity, declarativeness, etc. in the Semitic languages; reflexivity in Russian; passivity, reciprocity, reflexivity and various forms of modality in Turkish. All these categories are expressed by facultative formative elements; if we eliminate them from a sentence (taking into consideration the morphophonemic changes which they automatically entail), the grammaticalness of the sentence is not disturbed. We should distinguish between the facultative use of an element in a given sentence[4] and the facultativeness of an element in a language (i.e. in any sentence of the language in question). We would consider primarily the latter case.

We shall call the non-facultative formative elements *obligatory*.

---

[4]   We can obviously treat the difference between a preposition and a homonymous adverb (*I looked at him* — *He was looked at*) in English, as a difference between the obligatory and facultative use of one and the same element. Indeed, the use of the element in the prepositional function is obligatory, but the use of the same element without a following word is facultative [the facultative element is stressed as it (unlike the obligatory element) conveys information that is not obvious from the remaining elements in the sentence].

In the following analysis attention is focused on obligatory formative elements, i.e. it is the minimum conditions of grammaticalness of a sentence that are principally considered. It should be noted, however, that the possibility of inserting facultative elements can always be considered. The classes of the obligatory formative elements express certain *indispensable categories* — i.e. information which needs to be present in the sentences of a language.[5]

0.3. *Equivalence* — Two elements (combinations of elements) are equivalent if they are interchangeable in any sentence of a given language without disturbing the grammaticalness of the sentence. It is assumed that once we know a language, the relations of equivalence for that language are known. In other words, if one knows a certain sentence of a given language and the relations of equivalence proper to that language, one is able to produce different combinations of elements with the assurance that in the corpus of that language there will occur at least one sentence corresponding in its structure to the deliberately generated combination. Thus the majority of sentences possible in a language can be formed.[6]

Two mutually exclusive types of equivalence are to be distinguished:

1) The equivalence on the basis of which it is possible to effect the contraction and expansion of a sentence. The relations of equivalence of that type are expressed as $YZ \leftrightarrow Z$, i.e. one part of the formula includes the other; we shall say that component Y (which is not repeated in both parts of the formula) *modifies*

---

[5]　It can be shown that the *zero* element (the informative absence of an element) can be singled out only from among obligatory formative elements. Indeed, only on condition that a certain category is necessarily present in the sentences of a language (being an indispensable category of the given language), the mere absence of a concrete element expressing this category specifies its meaning: and vice versa: the absence of an element is only then informative, if we assume that the category designated by this element must be necessarily expressed in some way.

[6]　A certain part of the sentences are formed with the aid of supplementary grammatical transformations (one-sided transformations of sentences). Thus are formed the sentences with inversion, ellipsis, hypotaxis, etc. Such sentences will be excluded from the discussion; it is assumed that their examination is less essential for the analysis of the structure of a language.

component Z (repeated in both parts of the formula). For instance, formula $AN \leftrightarrow N$ means that the noun may be modified by unlimited number of adjectives and v.v., the combination of a noun with adjectives may be reduced to the noun alone.[7]

2) The equivalence on the basis of which we may effect substitution. For instance, the equivalence of the elements in a word and of the words in a sentence; the equivalence $Nless \leftrightarrow A$ (in English); $(V + participial\ index)$ A (in various languages).

The relations of the former type can be regarded as more significant for the general characterization of a language.

The relations of equivalence in a language may be described on the level of concrete elements and the level of classes. The equivalence of the concrete elements is postulated (can be given merely by listing the individual correspondances of equivalent elements); the equivalence of the classes is given in the form of general *rules of equivalence*.

It is the rules of equivalence for contraction and expansion that will be considered in what follows.

In all languages, apparently, the rule of equivalence exists for contraction and expansion: $Z\alpha Z \leftrightarrow Z$ (where Z may be an element or a combination of elements, and α a conjunction[8]), i.e. in any language a sentence may be expanded to any length by means of conjunctions, and vice versa, any combination with conjunctions may be reduced to a part of this combination. As we may assume

---

[7] We may note that the consecutive contraction determines the grammatical understanding (i.e. the comprehension of the function of concrete elements on the grammatical level). Correspondingly a possibility of a different understanding is determined by the possibility of applying a different order of contractions.

Accordingly, if we say that a certain grammatical structure (i.e. structural sequence in a language) is *polysemantic*, this means that it can be subjected to various (as to the order) operations. For polysemantic structures we can often find at least one sentence in speech that may be understood in different ways, for instance, the English sentence *He gave up smoking* (structure *NVVing* may be understood in two ways, the different interpretations depending on whether *smoking* is apprehended as syntactically bound up with *gave up* or with *he* : *gave up smoking* → *gave up* or *he ... smoking* → *he*.

[8] Conjunctions may be defined as formative elements that connect equivalent elements or combinations in such a way that the group formed (conjunctional combination) is equivalent to any of the initial components.

that conjunctions are present in any language, their existence in separate languages or languages types will not be specially mentioned in the characterization of a language or a language type. However, the possibility to contract and expand by means of conjunctions will be taken into consideration.

0.4. *The function* — In accordance with the above we say that a certain unit modifies another one if the latter can be expanded by the former. In a somewhat different — and a more general — sense a unit of a certain class x is said to modify a unit of another class y if x never appears without y, while y can occur without x[9]. (In that sense, for instance, a formative element can be said to modify a root.)

Now we shall say that we know the function of a certain unit (be it an element, a word, etc.), if we know what it can modify, or be modified by, in the language in question. The function of a grammatical unit in a language often may be described in terms of relations of equivalence (those of contraction and expansion).[10]

0.5. *The word* — If we designate a class of root elements by X, and classes of obligatory formative elements by n, m...,[11] we can regard the structure of every sentence of a language as the sequence of those symbols (in general the *structure* — of a word, a sentence, etc. — is defined as a sequence of classes). The function of the elements (of the combination of elements) can always be indicated.

Let us define the word as a sequence consisting of a root element plus certain obligatory formative elements within the same sentence which are in direct functional relationship with the root (i.e. as the structure of type Xn). Examples of words are: *stola* "table" (gen.), *stolom* "table" (instr.), *k stolu* "to the table" (dat.), *have done*

---

[9] See J. H. Greenberg, *Essays in linguistics* (New York, 1957), p. 14.
[10] Note that the relations of substitution indicate the equality of functions (in contraction ans expansion). It follows that the indication of contraction and expansion suffices for the description of the function of a given unit.
[11] It is convenient to regard empty elements as classes, consisting of one element.

(where the elements -*a*, -*om*, *k* — *u*, *have* — *ed* are "listed" in a language and are obligatory).

Words in different languages may be expanded both by facultative formative elements and by root elements. For instance, the Chukot *ny-tur-ten'-tejky-kinet* "newly-goodly-[they]do", the English *a stone wall*, the Russian *stolik* "small table" and the Arabic *ḥammada* "[he] praised much" — are expansions of the words *ny-tejky-kinet* "[they] do", *a wall*, *stol* "table", *ḥamida* "[he] praised";[12] these are, then, longer sequences than words.

The determination of the word is useful for the description of many languages but not for all: there are languages which have no words in the proposed sense. The concept of word is useful, particularly because it enables us in the case of commutation to change one complex of elements into another in bulk instead of in parts.

0.5.1.   *Word classes* — The words of a language fall into classes. Structure *Xn* which is proper to a certain word determines the composition of all the words of the class. They are formed in accordance with the structure by substituting the possible values of the class of root element *X* (the values of *X* being by definition infinite) as well as all possible values of the class of formative element *n*.

In every class the function of that class is overtly expressed (it is clear, that it must be expressed in formative elements, for the root elements of words are not distinguished on the level described): if in some two classes the function would not be expressed (or would be similarly expressed) then these two classes would coincide. Thus, the function of a word is defined by the class to which it belongs. The function of the word (the belonging of the word to this or that class) may be expressed by means of a class of interchangeable formative elements carrying some indispensable category (specific to the given class of words in opposition to others —

---

[12]   As can be seen, the proposed concept of word differs from the conventional one. The usual concept of word will be described later as the combination of a root element and formative elements of type II 1 that are connected with it (see below 2.2.1).

for instance, the categories of number, person) or by means of an empty element.[13] On the grammatical level the latter does not convey any information but the expression of the function of the word.

The function of a class can be described by the rules of equivalence for contraction and expansion which apply to this class.

A. EXPLICATION OF THE TERMS OF THE TRADITIONAL MORPHOLOGICAL CLASSIFICATION OF LANGUAGES ON THE BASIS OF THE ABOVE CONCEPTS

1. *Preliminary Remarks.*

A fundamental deficiency in the traditional morphological classification is the vagueness of terminology and the confusion of different criteria of classification (the desire to classify simultaneously according to various criteria and to combine several concepts in one term). Therefore it is possible to define the same languages in different ways. This may result, for instance, in the cases of confusion of incorporating and agglutinative languages;[14] incorporating and amorphous ones;[15] inflexional and agglutina-

---

[13] For instance, elements, designating the function of an adverb (Russ. *-o*, esper. *-e*, Engl. *-ly*, Fr. *-ment*); gerund forms; Esper. *-a*, *-o* designating the function of an adjective and substantive; numerous elements forming a noun from a verb in Turkish etc.

[14] Thus the Aleutian language was regarded as incorporating and as agglutinative (cf. V. I. Ioxel'son, *Unanganskij (aleutskij) jazyk* [The Unangian (aleutian) language] (= *Jazyki i pis'mennost' narodov Severa*, III, Moscow-Leningrad, 1943); G. A. Menovščikov, *Eskimossko-aleutskie jazyki* [Eskimo-Aleutian languages] (= *Mladopis'mennye jazyki narodov SSSR*, Moscow-Leningrad, 1959). This can also be applied to the Eskimo language.

[15] *See* V. Z. Panfilov, "K voprosu ob inkorporirovanii" [On the problem of incorporation], *Voprosy jazykoznanija*, 1954, 6, where the author identifies incorporation and juxtaposition. At the same time the features of amorphous languages are sometimes regarded as incorporations (see A. I. Ivanov, E. D. Polivanov, *Grammatika sovremennogo kitajskogo jazyka* [Grammar of contemporary Chinese] (Moscow, 1930), pp. 240-263.

tive languages;[16] agglutinative and amorphous languages,[17] etc.[18]

Nevertheless, the traditional morphological classification certainly has a rational core. Introducing a precise terminology (as E. Sapir did) and changing it according to some principles stated above, we may obtain a reliable way to describe and divide languages, proceeding from their structure.

A fundamental assumption is that in various languages certain uniform relations are expressed by different means. In some languages they are expressed consistently, for instance, by word-order. In other languages there are different ways of expression, e.g. word order, affixes, prepositions,[19] combination of affixes and prepositions, etc.). Should we succeed in reducing all these various means to one (for instance, word order), then the problem of a metalanguage as the basis for the classification of languages would be solved.

This should form the subject of later discussion, but first we must support our assumption by the typological examination of elements in various languages.

2. *Classification of the Elements*

2.1. As a result of the operations which were discussed above, we are dealing with structures representing sentences of various lan-

---

[16] Semitic languages, which are traditionally regarded as inflexional, are more and more regarded as agglutinative (see I. A. Mel'čuk, "O termine 'vnutrennjaja fleksija' v svjazi s aggljutinaciej", ["On the term 'inner flexion' in connection with agglutination", *Ponjatie aggljutinacii i aggljutinativnogo tipa jazykov*, (theses of essays at the conference) (Leningrad, 1961); C. E. Bazell, *op. cit.*, p. 17. At the same time there are some good grounds to regard the Bantu languages (traditionally classified as agglutinative) as inflexional (report made by N. V. Oxotina on the conference mentioned).

[17] Thus, A. Sommerfelt assumes that in Aranta (often placed with the agglutinative languages) parts of speech are not distinguished and he talks about the independent meaning of the suffixes of that language (*see* A. Sommerfelt, *La Langue et la Société* (Oslo, 1938), pp. 75, 109, 187.

[18] Esperanto may be defined as analytical, agglutinative or amorphous — to some extent a remarkable fact, as L. L. Zamenhof composed his language proceeding from the data of inflexional languages, but he developed their possibilities to the utmost, disregarding all kinds of limitations.

[19] The difference between an affix and a preposition is defined later (2.2.1).

guages. These structures are certain sequences of classes of elements I (root elements) and II (formative elements).[20]

Elements I and II are in a certain way combined with each other. Elements I can by definition be combined with a concrete list of elements (II), while elements II can be combined with any element of the class of root elements. Thus elements II are marked and serve as the indipensable grammatical mould of the sentences of language.

2.2.   We shall compare the elements of different languages by their functional meaning, i.e. by applying the criterion: "what do they modify (or are modified by)" or "what are they combined with".

2.2.1.   Elements II are divided into two mutually exclusive groups:[21]

Group II 1. Elements II 1 modify a word without modifying any combination equivalent to that word. Thus the expansion of a word by equivalent combinations may take place (at least in one instance) outside the complex modified by the elements of this group. For instance, a) Elements II1 in combination with a root: *stol*-A↔*bol'š*-OGO *stol*-A↔*stol*-A *i stul*-A, etc. "table" (gen.), "big table" (gen.), "table and chair" (gen.) b) Elements II2 in combination with a sequence: root + formative (i.e. a word): *exal*-A↔*xoroš*-O *exal*-A↔*exal*-A *i čital*-A, etc. "[she] went", "[she] went well", "[she] went and read".

In the examples the element -A modifies only the word to which it refers, but it does not modify the whole combination, regarded as an equivalent; in fact, expansion in terms of equivalent relations presupposes in this case either the repetition of this element or the introduction of some other elements connected with it. Other words are in the same way modified by elements II1. This case is represented by the structure

$$Zn \leftrightarrow Z_1 n_1 Zn \leftrightarrow Z_2 n_2 \alpha Zn \ldots,$$

[20]   By the definition of 'structure', *see* 0,5.
[21]   The following classification of formative elements is borne out by examples from various languages in the appendix (*see* appendix).

where *n* is an element II1, and *Z* may be a root or a word (a combination of a root with a formative element).

group II2: elements which modify a word as well as any equivalent combination (thus the expansion by equivalent combinations always takes place inside the complex modified by elements II2). For instance: a) Elements II2 in combination with a root: Chukot: NY-*lkyt*-KINET$\leftrightarrow$NY-*jyk-y-lkyt*-KINET$\leftrightarrow$NY-*gytg-y-jyk-y-lkyt*- KINET, etc. "[they] go", "[they] go fast", "[to the] lake [they] go fast". b) Elements II2 in combination with a sequence: root + formative (i.e. a word). Russian: NA-*stol-e*$\leftrightarrow$NA *xoroš-em* *stol-e*$\leftrightarrow$NA *stol-e i stul-e*, etc., "on the table (prep.)", "on the good table", "on the table and the chair".

In both cases the capitalized element II2 (the Chukot confix *ny-kinet* meaning the 3rd p. pl. II pres. tense and the Russian preposition *na*) introduces a root (or a sequence: root + formative, i.e. a word), which may in its turn be expanded by equivalent combinations. It is essential that the element II2 need not be repeated and modifies the whole group.[22]

This case is represented by the structure

$$Zn \leftrightarrow ZZn \leftrightarrow ZZZn \ldots,$$

where *n* is an element II2 and *Z* can be a root or a word.[23]

A formative element is recognized as element II1, if it can be

---

[22] An element II2 may also be facultatively repeated; then the question can be put thus: given expression $Z_1 n Z_2 n Z_3 n$ etc, will expression $Z_1 Z_2 Z_3 n$ (where *Z* is a root or a word) be grammatical?. In Turkish we may say *Çocuk*LAR, *kadın*LAR *ve ihtiyar*LAR (children, women and aged), but just as correct is the expression: *Çocuk, kadın ve ihtiyar*LAR, where the exponent of the plural -*lar* refers to the entire group. This also applies to prepositions in many languages which may be repeated, but may also be used once.

[23] The criterion indicated ("what does the given element modify" — i.e. does it refer to one word or to the entire combination) can easily be checked in the following way: let $Y \leftrightarrow ZY$, where *Z* may be a root or a word, and *Y* a word of structure *Xn*; if by a change in the meaning of *n* (substitution of other elements of class *n*) *Z* remains unchanged, we may draw the conclusion, that *n* modifies the entire combination *ZY*; if this is true for any combination equivalent to *Y*, this means that *n* is an element II2. If we can find a case where *Z* changes accroding to a change of *n*, we conclude that *n* modifies *Y* only, i.e. *n* is an element II1 (obviously in this case *Z* can only be a word, not a root).

proved that it does not belong to group II2. Conversely, the recognition of a formative element as element II2 calls for verification by means of all equivalence rules adopted for the language in question (thus, the element -A of the Russian *stol*-A "table", (gen.) may modify combination *stol*-A *učitelja* "the table (gen.) of the teacher (gen.)", which is equivalent to *stol*-A; however, it does not follow that -*a* is an element II2 (for instance, the combination *xoroš*-EGO *stol*-A "the good table (gen.)" contradicts this). In this way the elements II2 are marked among the formative ones.

To elements II2 belong:

The English article (it may define not only a class of nouns *N*, but also any combination equivalent to *N*: thus, given *aN* (*a choice*) and knowing, that *AN*↔*N*, we may form the combination *a AN* (*a happy choice*.) In the same way behave the articles of many languages, but not all: the Arabic article belongs to group II1 — it must be repeated in the case of agreement when expanding *N* to the equivalent *NN* (cf. Arabic 'AR*rağulu*↔'AR*rağulu-Lmarīdu* and English THE *man*↔THE *sick man*);

the Russian formative element *budu* (forming the future tense in combination with an infinitive: cf. *budu čitat'*↔*budu mnogoči tat'*↔ *budu čitat' i pisat'*, etc. "([I] shall read", [I] shall read much", "[I] shall read and write") and in the same way the so-called "auxiliary verbs" in many languages;

prepositions and postpositions in many languages, but not in all: for instance the French prepositions belong to elements II1 (cf. *à la table*↔*à la bonne table* but *à la table et à la chaise* (the preposition needs be repeated in the last phrase — otherwise this phrase is not equivalent to the initial one));[24]

---

[42] We may assume that in Russian too, the preposition was once an element II1. Cf. the repetition of the preposition in bylinas and old documents (A. A. Šaxmatov wrote that the repetition of the preposition in the Dvina documents occurs "before every or almost every word dependent on it", remarking, that the preposition is not repeated before an attribute, only when "this attribute is joined with a noun to a more or less constant combination", *see* A. A. Šaxmatov, *Issledovanie o dvinskix gramotax XV v.* [Investigation into the Dvina documents] (Sankt Peterburg, 1903), pp. 139-140. The repetition of the preposition remains in folk-lore language and in some dialects (*see* N. P. Grinkova, "Nekotorye slučai povtorenija predlogov v kirovskix dialextax", [Some cases of repetition

many formative elements of the Turkish language (cf. *ne yiyor, ne içiyor, ne de söylijor*DU "he did not eat, nor drink or speak", where the element *-du* (exponent of the past tense) modifies all the three verb forms, connected by a conjunction (*ne ... ne ... ne de*));

the formative elements of incorporating languages. Generally speaking "*incorporation*" (as a grammatical means) may be defined through the presence of elements II2; whereas "incorporating" (a language characteristic) may be defined as a language with an incorporation of the roots (i.e. a language in which the elements II2 do not modify a combination of words, but combinations of roots).

Thus, the structure *XXn*, characteristic for incorporating languages, where *n* is grammatical form, correlates typologically with, e.g. the English structure *of XX* (*of stone wall*), i.e. the affixes of incorporating languages do not differ as to their function from the English (or other) prepositions (and in the same way from the English articles etc.).

2.2.2. The elements of class I (root elements) can be classified in accordance with their combinability with formative elements.

Group I1: elements of this group are combined with elements II1 and II2 (and thus words are formed):

the Russian: *stol-* in *stol-*A; the English: A *wall* (the article is the exponent of the noun); the Chukot: NY-*tejky*-KINET ("they do" (the capitalized affixes are of the 3rd p. pl. II pres. tense)), etc.

Group I2: elements of this group are not directly combined with formative elements.

For instance:

a) the root elements of amorphous languages, which have no grammatical modification;

b) the adjoining root elements of incorporating languages, by which we can expand structure *Xn* to *XXn*, to *XXXn*, etc. (where *X* is a root, and *n* a grammatical form; cf. the example cited from the Chukot language. In this case it is not only one root that is modified by formative elements, but a whole complex of roots.

For instance: A *stone wall*; NY-*tur-ten'-tejky*-KINET "newly, goodly, they do". In this complex of roots a certain root belongs necessarily to type I1, i.e. can be used in the same grammatical form independently (here: *wall, tejky*) — otherwise the whole complex of roots should have been treated as one root (type I1). The remaining ones only acquire their grammatical form in combination with this root in a given sentence.

2.3. Formative elements can be divided into *analytical* and *synthetical*, depending on whether they express one grammatical category or more. An analytical element does not express more than one grammatical category, whereas a synthetical element expresses several grammatical categories at a time. This corresponds to the division into agglutination and fusion, given by E. Sapir.[25]

3. *A Classification of Languages in Terms of Different Component Elements and an Attempt to Build Up 'a priori' Constructions*

3.1. Various languages can be characterized by the presence or absence of certain groups of elements. Thus we can obtain a general classification of languages, in terms of which it is possible to interpret the traditional morphological classification.

3.1.1. Thus, incorporating languages are *a priori* characterized by the absence of elements II1, and the presence of elements II2 (i.e. all formative elements belong to type II2).

3.1.2. In a "completely amorphous" language only elements of type I2 should exist. As is known, so far no language has been found to be completely amorphous (i.e. a language with no formative elements whatsoever, all relations being expressed exclusively by the order of units). A language of this kind is hardly possible, as it would obviously be incapable of fulfilling the communicative function.[26]

Indeed, a sentence of such a language must be a string of type

[25] E. Sapir, *Jazyk* [Language]. (Moscow-Leningrad, Socegkiz, 1934), p. 103.
[26] *See* P. S. Kuznecov, *Morfologičeskaja klassifikacija jazykov* [A morphological classification of languages] (Moscow, Izd-vo MGU, 1954), p. 14.

$X_1 X_2 X_3 X_4$ ... (where the X-es are elements I2). Here the number of elements in a string can not apparently be firmly established in any language (which is due to the fact that there are relations of equivalence in a language, according to which any sentence may be expanded to any length).

It follows that the function of every element X in the sequence $X_1 X_2 X_3 X_4$ ... is not clear, i.e. one can't say what it modifies, and consequently the order of contractions is not obvious. The sentence becomes polysemantic (according to the definition of polysemantism (see 0.3, note 7).

When a priori constructing such an abstract scheme of an amorphous language the following solutions suggest themselves:

A. To impose certain restrictions on the length or the sentence (number of elements) — be it only in so far as to decide whether the number should be odd or even. In that case it would be possible to define the function of every part of the sentence by its position in the sentence. The existence of such languages is hardly possible. The requirement to establish the number of elements in a sentence contradicts the rules of equivalence which are given for every language. By definition every (root) element can be expanded to any length possible (by equivalent combinations). If we require this element to be expanded only in a, e.g., even or odd way, we would have to insert some special (empty) elements, i.e. formative ones. We would then inevitably arrive at a language of another structure (not entirely amorphous)[27] and not in the simplest way (the establishing of the number of root elements in a sentence is not necessary then).

It is interesting to note, however, that in classical Chinese (Wen jan) the sentences sometimes conform to a fixed length being constructed from a strictly limited number of hieroglyphs (e.g. 4, 6, 8, or 3, 5, 7, 9, 11, 13).[28]

[27]   On the other hand, if we require a certain element to entail obligatorily some other (not empty) element in such a way that only the total of both these elements represents the semantic value, these two elements would be one morpheme, i.e. one element.

[28]   See V. S. Kolokolov, *Kratkij kitajsko-russkij slovar'* [Concise Chinese-Russian dictionary] (Moscow, OGIZ, 1935), p. 672.

It is not impossible that to some extent this characteristic is also conditioned by requirements of communication.

B. To insert special elements indicating the order of contractions (the function of these elements is similar to the function of brackets in mathematical notation). This is the case in Chinese, which possesses elements II2 (e.g. element *dy*, which indicates that any group, modified by it, is contracted to one).

C. To invest certain roots with a formative function, so that their presence becomes obligatory in the sentence. In this case we are dealing with words (according to the definition of word — see 0.5). Such is apparently the case in Aranta, where the elements which make the obligatory grammatical form of words (by expressing certain indispensable categories) do not lose their own meanings and may be used independently. Thus from a certain point of view a sentence in Aranta may be regarded as consisting entirely of roots (I2), which means that this language is amorphous. On the other hand its words may be regarded as roots modified by formative elements (in so far as these elements can be "listed" in the language). Proceeding from the semantic concept of the words "root" and "formative element", Aranta should be defined as amorphous (but with words), for its sentences consist of roots — completely autosemantic elements which can be used independently. But if we proceed from the assumed concept of formative elements as marked elements, which are given by "listing" in a language (*see* 0.2.1), then Aranta is not an amorphous language (some of its words are marked and represent elements of type II).

Thus, a language without formative elements ("completely amorphous") is apparently impossible. Each language must possess certain formative elements indicating the order of contraction of components in a sentence (without this, the sentences of a language could be interpreted in many contradictory ways and the language itself would not be communicative). In an amorphous language such elements do not express any additional information and possess a highly abstract meaning being functionally similar to brackets in mathematical notation. Elements of this kind may be thus

called *bracket elements*. It can be shown that these elements
should belong to type II2.[29]

3.1.3. We may conjecture the existence of a "completely inflexional" language, in which all elements belong either to type II1
or to type I1, which is supplementary to type II1 (i.e. all formative
elements would have to represent the inflexion of type -*a* in *stol*-A,
but in no case a pre- or postposition).

In such a language no elements II2 are conceivable, which ensures
the absence of incorporation. At the same time, all words here
are connected either by agreement or government, never being in
juxtaposition — hence the absence of amorphousness.

3.1.4. Agglutinative languages are distinguished from inflexional
languages by another criterion — by the criterion of analytism and
synthetism (see 2.3.); apparently, their formative elements may also
represent either type II1 or type II2, but each of them definitely
expresses only one grammatical category.

3.2. The classification of languages on the basis of the assumed
element classification is made more difficult by the fact, that very
seldom the elements of only one type are represented in languages.
For instance, in Russian there are, apart from elements II1 (corresponding with its inflectiveness) also elements II2 (prepositions);
Turkish has, besides elements I1, elements I2, etc.[30] In every
language, however, we can see a preferred distribution of elements

---

[29]   It is essential to note that the occurrence of a bracket element in a definite
position in a sentence can not be formally predicted, i.e. we cannot say that the
grammaticalness of the sentence conditions the presence of this element in this
particular position.   Consequently it is not the question of a certain root (of
type I 1) requiring an obligatory grammatical modification by a bracket element
(it follows that the combination of a word and a bracket element cannot be
treated as a word).

We could give a more precise definition of word now as a root of type I 1
in combination with obligatory formative elements that modify it within a
sentence.

[30]   A language may often contain elements of different kinds, depending on the
fact whether they relate to *N* or to *V*. E.g., in Russian elements II2 (prepositions) relate to *N*; in English and German elements II1 relate to V, etc. We
may take this into account when typologically describing and comparing
various languages.

of a certain type (and thus we can characterize the language). Even more significant for the characterization of a language is the absence of elements of a certain type.

With this in mind, we can describe the different types of the traditional morphological classification of languages, using the element classification.

For *incorporating* languages, the predominance of elements II2, I1, I2, is significant; *elements II1 are absent.*

For *amorphous* languages, the predominance of elements I2 is significant; *elements I1 are absent.*

Inflexional and *agglutinative* languages, possessing mainly the types II1, II2, and I1, are distinguished by the use of synthetical and analytical elements respectively; *elements I2 are absent.*[31]

We can see, that the traditional morphological classification of languages distinguishes the languages by applying different criteria: thus the differentiation between incorporating languages and inflexional languages is based on the criterion of presence or absence of elements II1; the differentiation of agglutinative and inflexional languages on the criterion of analytism or synthetism of formative elements; amorphous languages are distinguished by the absence of indispensable categories.

The different principles of division used in the traditional morphological classification of languages (in terms of different kinds of elements) are shown in the graph on page 48.

3.3. The suggested approach enables us to account for some causes of the confusion of language-types in the morphological classification (*see* 1).

3.3.1. Incorporating and agglutinative languages can be characterized by the presence of elements II2; the possibility of confusion is illustrated by the intersection of squares in the graph

---

[31] We may distinguish *a priori* the group of languages in which elements II2 are absent; we may also divide incorporating languages according to their use of synthetical or analytical elements. In the traditional morphological classification, however, these groups of languages are not distinguished; apparently, these distinctions are in fact typologically not particularly characteristic.

Root (I) elements	Subsidiary elements (II)		
	Synthetical	Analytical	
	= = = = = = = =	○ ○ ○ ○ ○ ○ ○ ○ ○ ○	Of type 1 (II 1)
	+ + + + + + + +	○ ○ ○ ○ +○+ + + + + ○ ○ ○ ○ +○+ + + + + ○ ○ ○ ○ +○+ + + + + ○ ○ ○ ○	Of type 2 (II 2)

	+ + + + + +	○ ○ ○ ○ ○ ○	= = = = = =
Amorphous	Incorporating	Agglutinative	Inflexional

There are no adjectives in most agglutinative languages: the attribute representing the pure root X_1 is juxtaposed to the determined $X_2 n$ (as in Turkish). Then the formative element n in $X_1 X_2 n$ (which modifies the word to be determined) can be regarded as modifying the entire complex $X_1 X_2$ and the whole phenomenon is interpreted as an incorporation.

3.3.2. Incorporating and amorphous languages both have elements I2 (pure roots in juxtaposition), we can therefore find examples which can be interpreted in two ways. For incorporating languages, however, the presence of elements I1, which require obligatory grammatical form, is essential.

3.3.3. Inflexional (analytic) and agglutinative languages are similar in so far as the elements II2 of an agglutinative language do not differ functionally from the prepositions (postpositions) of an inflexional language.

3.3.4.   A language of the Aranta type can be regarded as both agglutinative and amorphous. The confusion arises from the reasons mentioned above (3.1.2.): the criteria of root definition overlap. If we approach the root from a purely semantic point of view or according to the possibility of independent use, the Aranta language is amorphous. But if we define the root as a class of elements which cannot be "listed" (cf. 0.2.), the grammatical elements of that language are formative elements; then its relation to the agglutinative languages is obvious. In both approaches, it can be pointed out that in Aranta the word does exist (this would distinguish Aranta from a typical amorphous language, even if we regard Aranta as generally amorphous).

B.   DETERMINATION OF THE STRUCTURE OF AN ÉTALON LANGUAGE FOR TYPOLOGICAL COMPARISON BY USING THE TERMINOLOGY EVOLVED SO FAR

4.   *The Interrelation Between Various Types of Languages — Stepwise Conversion of Languages of One Type to Languages of Another One.*

4.1.   It is interesting to compare various languages according to the criterion of freedom or boundness of the elements in a string.

Let us take a certain string of elements (in a given language). We can present its structure if we replace concrete elements by symbols of classes to which they belong: X, n_1, n_2, etc. Each class then comprises a certain set of values, i.e. a set of interchangeable elements. The question then arises how far it is possible to interchange the elements inside a class, i.e. whether we can arbitrarily replace one element by another of the same scope of meanings without disturbing the grammaticalness of the sentence.

It turns out that this possibility exists to a different degree for different languages. In certain languages the meaning of one element is bound up with the meaning of another element in a string, i.e. the change of one element involves an obligatory corresponding change of another element.

Now, by definition the elements of type I (root elements) cannot be bound elements — in any case on the level described.[32] Only formative elements, expressing indispensable categories, can be bound ones. It is more convenient to deal with indispensable categories, instead of the elements themselves, i.e. with the information which is necessarily expressed in words as such. In the case of agreement this information is repeated.

4.2. Passing from the concrete formative elements to the meanings of the indispensable categories, we simultaneously pass from the synthetical structure of elements to the analytical one (from the inflexional structure to the agglutinative structure in terms of the traditional classification). This actually occurs in grammatical analysis, when, e.g., the word *stola* is analyzed as a "noun in the genitive singular" — the grammatical meanings, synthetically united in the element -*a*, are analyzed analytically. If exclusively agglutinative languages were the subject of typological investigation it would not be necessary to pass from elements to meanings, for elements here correlate unambigously to grammatical meanings and thus we can work directly with elements.

However languages with synthetical elements must be converted to the analytical form because the latter is a simpler subject to deal with. This is practically indispensable in comparative analysis of languages. As could be seen from the above example of the analysis of *stola*, this procedure actually takes place in all grammatical analyses, especially in the comparative one.

Passing from the concrete formative elements to the categorial meanings they express, we shall go on considering the latter as elements. In other words, we shall treat as elements symbols for indispensable categories. As a matter of fact, we can assume that we deal with elements of a certain language which is identical to the language under analysis, the only difference between them being the fact that the former language possesses analytical elements, while those of the latter language are synthetical.

It should be mentioned that conversion of this kind does not

[32]   The disregarding of all semantic restrictions has been stipulated before (0.1).

impair the condition of reversibility,[33] i.e. a reverse process is as much possible — from the analytical structure to the synthetical, by introducing certain supplementary rules (which indicate the combination of various grammatical meanings in concrete elements) without loss of information.[34]

Thus, *the structure of a language with analytical elements (an agglutinative language) appears as the structure of a metalanguage in relation to a corresponding language with synthetical elements (an inflected language).*[35] The agglutinative structure is actually used in this function in linguistic analysis — both by man and machine,[36] (provided there is no isomorphism between the two compared languages).[37]

4.3. Strings of elements in certain languages are bound by a compulsory repetition of a certain information. This is the case with agreement and government.

In fact, agreement is in essence merely the compulsory repetition of a certain information.[38] This information can be expressed by various elements, but a distributional analysis and a transition from

---

[33] *See* note 34 in the first part of the work.

[34] Cf. C. F. Shannon, "The redundancy of English", *Cybernetics* (Transactions of the 7th conference). (New-York, 1951), p. 157. The information is defined as the invariant in the reversible process of translation or coding.

[35] In fact, grammatical analysis of a synthetical language is produced in symbols of an analytical language; cf. the definition of *meta-* as given earlier (note 31 in the first part).

[36] For a machine translation between two languages (between inflexional languages and, even more so, between inflexional and agglutinative languages) it is necessary to make a table of the corresponding grammatical meanings of these languages, where the meanings must be expressed analytically.

[37] It is significant that without proper knowledge of a certain inflexional language the speaker usually changes it into a more agglutinative language (makes it more agglutinative). The speech of children makes an immediate example; on the other hand, certain agglutinative peculiarities of some Hittite texts are due to the fact that its writers were representatives of another (Luvian) language; cf. also the incorrect rendering of Sumerian words by Hittites (for instance, ANŠU. KUR. RA meš.ḫi.a, where *meš* and *ḫi.a* both indicate the plural which is impossible in Sumerian.

[38] We mean grammatical agreement (i.e. obligatory, independent of the meanings of root elements) as opposed to semantic agreement, which we find, e.g. in English, in Arabic, etc.

the elements to the information expressed anables us to treat these elements as allo-forms.

Generally speaking, government is similar to agreement. Government in the proper sense (the requirement of a case according to the preposition in the European languages; the requirement of a definite verbal mood according to the particle in Arabic; the requirement of a genitive case with the negative form of a verb in Russian) represents agreement in a governed construction in the sense that a certain information which had already been expressed is repeated (not infrequently by using elements of different classes: II1 and II2, which are not identified by distributional analysis).[39] As will be seen below this repeated information can be placed "outside the brackets", thus being attached to the governing element. When this is not the case (i.e. when the information is not redundant and cannot be predicted on the level in question, e.g. in the Russian sequence VN several cases of N — accusative, dative or instrumental — being equally possible), then the syntactical relations will not be regarded as government.

All regularly repeated elements (or meanings[40]) may be placed "outside the brackets". Then the elements are no longer bound (every element in a string can be replaced by another of the same meaning).

For instance:[41] *Malen'kaja devočka pobežala v les* "the young girl ran into the wood".

[39] In the ideal case (if government is always and unambiguously expressed) the governing and governed morphemes form one element; thus, the preposition and the exponent of the case governed by it form a confix, which may consist of element II2 (the preposition; it can modify the entire following group, which may be expanded by equivalent combinations) and of element II1 (the exponent; it modifies a concrete root element and accordingly can be repeated when the group is expanded). Cf.: *k lesu (mXn)*, *k bol'šomu lesu (mX₁n₁Xn)* [towards the wood, towards the large wood], where m is an element II2 and n an element II1.

[40] By carrying out a distributional analysis and reducing synthetical elements to analytism, these terms really designate one and the same thing.

[41] In the examples the vertical lines mark off the nuclei of the string; the grammatical characteristics of the roots precede them or the combination in brackets; the independent parts of the string are marked off by commas. The government of a preposition is indicated at once, after a hyphen (it is thus placed "outside

/fem./sg./ [nom./(X/X), /perf.asp./past tns./X], *v*-/acc./(masc./sg./ X)/

In grauer Vorzeit besiedelten die Polynesier die südöstlichen Inseln /*in*-/dat./ [sg./(X/X)], /pl./ [past tns/X,/nom./stat.determ./(X)]/, acc./pl./stat.determ./(X/X)/

Se fué el padre del joven a casa del moro rico /3 pers./sg./{past tns/X,/stat.determ./[sg./masc./X/*de*/stat.determ. /(sg./masc./X)]},/*a*/ [fem./X/*de*/stat.determ./sg./masc./(X/X)]/

The procedure of placing outside brackets does not impair with the requirement of reversibility. Therefore, a similar operation may be applied when compiling programs in machine translation (before the brackets we find the prescript: "agreement according to certain features").

Now that this procedure is carried out, the elements are free in a string: indeed we can arbitrarily change elements inside a class without disturbing the grammaticalness.

Analizing the transformed strings, we may find that they represent a language of a different typology (compared with the initial strings). Their structure resembles the structure of incorporating languages.

Indeed, the elements placed "outside the brackets" have become elements of type II2, for they modify a certain group or any combination equivalent to that group.[42]

So we have come to the scheme of incorporating languages. As a matter of fact, the combination of the elements placed "outside the brackets" with those that are left inside the brackets can be regarded as "words" of these languages, modified by elements II2; outside the brackets are indispensable categories which characterize these words. By means of these indispensable categories we are able to discern the function of the "word" (as in a real language). Thus, in Russian the characteristics of case and number (gender) placed outside the brackets signify that in the brackets we find a

---

the brackets"). Brackets are used when the construction can be expanded by equivalent relations (i.e. in cases of placing outside the brackets as well as in those cases when elements II 2 take part).

[42] The reason of putting brackets after elements of type II2 (prepositions, in particular) in the above notation can be evident now.

noun or its equivalent combination (for instance an attributive
combination: adjective — noun); the characteristics of number
(gender) and person signify the combination: noun — verb in the
present tense; the characteristics of number (gender) and the absence of the characteristics of person signify the combination:
noun — verb in the past tense; in the Bantu languages the characteristics of nominal class are placed outside the brackets. A
similar analysis can also be carried out for other languages as
well.[43]

Thus, *the structure of a language with elements II2 (an incorporating language) appears as the structure of a metalanguage with
respect to a corresponding language with synthetical elements (an
inflected language).*

4.4.   Let us examine what remains inside the brackets. This is:

1)   the information of the function of a word (which is a necessary condition).

For instance, the Esperanto *bonaj komencoj* (the structure *Xaj
Xoj →j(Xa Xo)* or *j AN)*); when the exponent of the plural (-j) has
been placed outside the brackets the roots and exponent of the
functions of the adjective -*a*- and the noun -*o*- (empty elements)
remain within the brackets.

In case, when there is no such exponent (within the brackets the
pure root remains, and all indispensable categories are placed outside the brackets), the information on the function (e.g. *A, V, N,
Adv.*) of this root cannot be lost (this information was obvious from
the exponents characterizing the root while it stil was part of the
word); this follows from the condition of reversibility. We can
use the order of elements to specify the function of the roots in
the brackets.

2)   Some particular categories (which is, however, optional).
For instance, the tense (aspect) of the verb or the case of the noun.

If we specify the function exclusively by order of elements and

---

[43]   The function of the characterization placed outside the brackets is analogous
to the functions of sharps and flats in music notation (in the key) or to the
functions of the quantifiers in the language of mathematical logic.

regard the remaining particular categories as not obligatory but facultative, we shall obtain within the brackets the structure of amorphous languages.

So we may conclude that an amorphous structure lies at the basis of any typologically possible structure. In other words, we may say that an amorphous structure is the *simplest* one — one in which some basic relations (invariant for all languages) are expressed in the most consistent way. At the same time other structures can be represented by introducing supplementary (complicating)[44] rules, namely: if we carry out the performed operations in inverse order — from simple to complex — the structure of any language can be characterized by the scheme:

---

amorphous structure + introduction of indispensable categories (through obligatory formative elements) + expansion of obligatory formative elements (through rules of government and agreement) + synthetism of elements

---

Thus, the types of the traditional morphological classification may be arranged in order of complexity: amorphous languages — incorporating languages — agglutinative language — inflexional languages.

Hence, *the structure of an amorphous language appears as the structure of a metalanguage with respect to a corresponding language of any type* (incorporating, agglutinative or inflexional). Now the structures of different languages can be presented according to the degrees of their proximity to the structure of the amorphous metalanguage (étalon language). The degree of proximity (or, in other words, the degree of complexity) is formally determined by the number of transformations from the structure of a given

[44] We assume a language to be more *complex*, the farther it is from the amorphous structure.

language to the structure of the étalon language (the amorphous structure).[45]

At the same time the suggested approach provides for describing different linguistic phenomena consecutively from simple to more complex. For instance, the construction $VN \leftrightarrow N$ (in Yukagir and Gilyak) — i.e. a verb, modifying a noun, — acquires a special functional expression in the European languages (participles). This correspondence is of the same kind as the correspondence of an infinitive with a preposition (French, Spanish) — to a gerund (in English), to a verbal noun (in Russian). In other words, what in some languages is designated by the word-order, is expressed in a special way in other languages (i.e. it acquires a certain formative element which, in combination with the root, signifies its function).

Thus, the suggested approach enables us to appraise individual phenomena of various languages as well as to classify languages as a whole in a general way.

5. *The Typological Appraisal of the Structural Phenomena of Different Languages*

5.1. As a result of the suggested analysis it will be possible to compare any two corresponding constructions of different languages ("corresponding" are those sentence structures of different languages that correspond to the same sentence when compared with the metalanguage) and to appraise one construction as the more simple, the other as the more complex. The appraisal is performed on the basis of the number of stages in the transformation from the structure of metalanguage to the analyzed structure.

Here, the complexity of the language structure can be shown by means of intralingual operations. As a result of these operations the complex structures disintegrate into amorphous structures plus

---

[45] When defining the degree of complexity of a structure it is necessary to take into account both the number of different transformational steps and the number of monotype transformations within each step. However, in order to obtain a more general typological characterization of a language it is possible to consider only the first factor.

some grammatical transformations. The number of these transformations determines the complexity of the structure in question.[46]
5.2. Let us give some examples:

1) the construction "attribute + determinatum" in English (*a
stone wall*), Turkish (*taş duvar* — literally "stone-wall") is simpler
than the corresponding Russian (*kamennaja stena* "stone wall").
The English and Turkish adjoining attributes correspond completely
with an amorphous construction; at the same time, the function of
the Russian adjective is formed (compared with an amorphous
structure) by means of the transformation of agreement.

What has been said about English and Turkish is to the same
extent applicable to the adjoining attributes of Mongolic, many
American Indian languages etc.

2) Incorporating has been defined above (2.2.1.) by the presence
of elements II2, which modifies a certain group as well as any
combination equivalent to it. In this sense incorporation is
characteristic of English and Chukot.

Indeed, many English formative elements apparently belong
to type II2.

Cf. *General out-of-joint* NESS *of the world. Sage they were, great
headnodders and "I-would-not-venture-to-do-a-thing-like-this"* ERS.[47]

In Chukot the formative elements also belong to type II2.

Cf. *Jarak* NY-*tke*-KEN "It smells in a yourta" *Jarak* NY-*čača-ynn-
y-tke*-KEN "In a yourta it smells nicely of fish".

Here the Chukot construction is simpler than the English: in
Chukot element II2 modifies the sequence of the roots, whose
functions are all represented by their order (which corresponds
completely to an amorphous structure); at the same time, elements
II2 modifies in English the sequence of words — i.e. the combination
of roots with certain indispensable categories specifying their

---

[46] When comparing two structures *A* and *B* it is not necessary to reduce them
to an amorphous structure. It is often sufficient to convert structure *A* to
structure *B*, indicating that *A* may be described through *B* plus some transformation, i.e. *B* represents a simpler structure.
[47] Capitalized are the elements II2.

function. Compared with Chukot, certain supplementary transformation is necessary for their description.

What has been said about Chukot applies to many American
Indian languages, and also to certain Caucasian languages.

3)   Similar relations exist between English and Russian prepositional constructions.

In both languages the preposition is an element II2 (as has been
determined above, see 2.2.1.).

In the English language, however, the prepositional construction
is mainly expanded by unformed root elements (which corresponds
to an amorphous structure), and in Russian by words.

Cf. *in a tall house — v vysokom dome.*

In Russian, therefore, a prepositional construction is more
complex than in English; it can be described through the English
construction with an addition of certain supplementary transformations.

What has been said about Russian can be applied to Latin,
German and Arabic, what has been said about English, to Turkish.

4)   The infinitive with preposition in French corresponds to the
-ing form in English (gerund or verbal noun) and to the verbal
noun in Russian.

Cf. *pour faire — for doing — dlja delanija.*

The French construction is simpler than the corresponding
English and Russian constructions (through it does not correspond
to an amorphous structure like the previous examples): the English
and the Russian infinitive can indeed be described through the
French infinitive, having stipulated the appearance of an empty
element (*-ing,* Russ. *-nie*) to a verb when it is combined with a
preposition.

The examples quoted demonstrate the relative complexity or
simplicity of the structural phenomena of various languages, and
also their isomorphism. Disposing of a sufficiently extensive number of languages, we can form a table of correspondences for the
structural phenomena of various languages from simple to complex.

Thus we can compare structural constructions of various languages. We can also compare the languages themselves on the

bases of their characteristic structural constructions.[48] Both tasks — i.e. a characterization of a given structural construction in a language and a general characterization of the language as a whole — would practically amount to the same if each language consisted of typologically homogeneous constructions. This is an ideal case (which can be conventionally assumed when constituing an abstract typological theory), but practically this does not hold true for most languages. Consequently a more detailed typological characterization presupposes the introduction of an additional basis of comparison. It seems reasonable to use comparison of equivalence rules in various languages as an additional basis of typological characterization since it can be generally assumed that a language is represented as a certain sentence + equivalence rules allowing to transform this sentence into all other sentences of the language. It will be seen that different systems of equivalence rules in a certain language determines the existence of different word classes in this language. Hence the presence of certain word classes in a language can serve as a typological characteristic of equivalence rules in this language. The comparison of word classes in different languages can thus serve as an additional basis of detailed typological classification. The problems which are connected with a comparison of this kind will be discussed below.

C. A SPECIAL (SUPPLEMENTARY)
ÉTALON LANGUAGE FOR THE COMPARISON
OF WORD CLASSES IN VARIOUS LANGUAGES

6. *Preliminary Remarks. Establishing the System
of Word Classes for a given Language*

6.1. We proposed earlier to build a typological classification of languages on the basis of comparison with a simple metalanguage. We will give an example of the application of a complex meta-

[48] The traditional morphological classification compares languages in this way (even if the shortcomings mentioned above are done away with), objects of comparison not being languages, but certain constructions which are especially characteristic for these languages (see p. 23 of the present work).

language to settle another, more specific, typological problem —-
that of the comparison of word classes in different languages.

A typological comparison of word classes requires a certain
invariant basis, i.e. it is necessary to ascribe certain invariant values
(abstract meanings) to word classes so as to be able to identify
word classes according to their meaning. This is exactly what
linguists do when they designate word classes of structurally different languages by the same terms (such as "nouns", "verbs",
"adjectives", etc.). Such a comparison however, is usually made on
the basis of semantic criteria (these criteria can formally be
described through lexical correspondences).

We can also identify the word classes of different languages on the
basis of the grammatical categories which they express (e.g., a word
expressing case will be identified as a noun; a word expressing
tense will be identified as a verb, etc.).[49] Such a comparison
necessarily presupposes, however a preliminary identification of
the grammatical categories expressed in various languages, i.e.
establishing a taxonomy of categories. Here we can find that in
certain languages there are no general categories whatsoever; and
so the general number of types of word classes increases.[50] Apart
from this, the method of identifying word classes on the basis of
identical categories expressed by them, considers only the morphological criterion. At the same time, it seems appropriate to identify
word classes on the basis of their identical functioning in a sentence
(since the morphological criterion was already applied while
distinguishing word classes within a language). In particular, one
might reasonably name that class "adjective" which modifies a

---

[49]   This method is used, in particular, in the following works: M. N. Peterson,
Sovremennyj russkij jazyk [Contemporary Russian] (Moscow, Bjuro zaočnogo
obučenija pri pedfake II MGU, 1929); O. V. Pletner, E. D. Polivanov, *Grammatika japonskogo razgovornogo jazyka* [A grammar of Spoken Japanese]
(= *Tr. Mosk. in-ta vostokovedenija im. Narimanova*, XIV) (1930).
[50]   It is equally possible to define categories (and accordingly identify the
categories of various languages) on the basis of their belonging to a certain
word class. E.g., the fact that this category belongs to a noun (elements
expressing this category belong to a noun) can be regarded as an essential feature
of the case; tense is characterized by the fact that it belongs to a verb, etc. Here
we must first, however, establish the taxonomy of the word classes.

noun (i.e. $AN \leftrightarrow N$), and "adverb" — that class that modifies a verb (or adjective), etc.[51]

Thus, it appears reasonable to distinguish between word classes within a language on the basis of differences in morphological structure (as was proposed in 0.5.1); then one can determine the functional value (meaning) of a word class on the basis of its combinability with the other word classes of the same language. The combinability of word classes is used to determine the relations of word classes in a separate language. After this, word classes of different languages can be compared and identified on the basis of adequate relations (which means an adequate function of a word class in respective languages). The combinability of a word class in a language can be described by indicating the rules of equivalence (for contraction and expansion) pertaining to this word class. Thus, *the meaning (functional value) of a certain word class is determined by a list of rules of equivalence which demonstrate its combinability with other word classes distinguished in the language.*

Let us first examine certain consequences of this thesis, investigating the word classes in one language (without their correlation with other classes in other languages, i.e. designating them in an arbitrary way).

6.2.   Suppose that in a language a series of word classes is distinguished (according to the principles laid down in 0.5.1.), which we will designate arbitrarily ($T. K. F. ...$). The meaning of every class is described as the list of rules of equivalence, which show its capacity to combine with other classes (thus the meaning of class Z is a finite set, consisting of rules of equivalence of type $YZ \leftrightarrow Z$ or $ZY \leftrightarrow Y$).

Let us examine some possible relations of meanings of word classes, belonging to one language. These relations can best be described by means of some elementary procedures of the theory of sets.

[51]   Note that all denominations of word classes in paragraph 6 are conventional. Indeed, we do not know yet the meanings of word classes and the object of their designation is only the indication (for clearness' sake) of the approximate correspondence of a given word class to a certain part of speech in the traditional grammar.

1. *The inclusion of the meanings of one class in another*: $K \subset T$. This means that the rules of equivalence of one class (T) include the rules of equivalence of another class (K); accordingly the meaning of class T covers the meaning of class K. A word class whose meaning is covered by the meaning of another class, can be called a *subclass* of the latter (we shall designate the subclasses of some class F as F', F'' etc.). These subclasses have a limited ability to combine, compared with corresponding classes they belong to; accordingly, the meaning of F' can be described through F (by giving the restricting rules).

For instance, in the Russian language the subclasses of the classes N and A are formed by the class of pronouns[52] and the class of numerals (their meanings can be correspondingly described by imposing certain restrictions on the combinability of N and A).

In certain languages a class of intransitive verbs is formally distinguished (e.g. in paleoasiatic languages), i.e. intransitive verbs are characterised by special formative elements different from those of transitive verbs. It is easy to show that in these languages the class of intransitive verbs is a subclass of the class of transitive verbs (which in its turn coincides as to its combinability with the general class of verbs).[53]

The system of word classes in a language can be described on different levels — on the level of basic classes and on the level of subclasses. The first level is more general — the second more detailed.

B. *The equality of the meanings of classes*: $T = K(T \subset K, K \subset T)$. This means that two word classes can be distinguished in a language, whose rules of equivalence coincide (they have the same ability to combine with other classes). In this case we shall identify these two classes.

For instance, in Russian two word classes of different structure

---

[52] Apparently, pronouns in English do not differ as to their use from nouns and, thus, do not form a separate subclass (cf. such expressions as *poor little me*, *the great ones of finance*, *a nothing*, etc.).

[53] Intransitive verbs of all languages can be regarded as a subclass of the class of verbs (transitive), distinguished morphologically (in the way indicated in 0.5.1. — as in the paleoasiatic languages) or formed artificially by modeling the semantics of a certain part of the verb.

are distinguished: V_1 — verbs in the present and future tense (of the structure Xn, where n is the class of formative elements denoting person — number) and V_2 — verbs in the past tense (of the structure Xm, where m is the class of formative elements denoting gender — number). These two classes coincide as to meaning (function), because the rules of equivalence, which characterize them, are identical (they have the same ability to combine with other word classes in Russian); therefore we identify them in one class V.

When describing the systems of word classes in a language it is reasonable to examine only word classes with different meaning.

C. *The union of the meanings of the classes:* $T+K=F$. I.e. the rules of equivalence of one class are equal to the logical sum of the rules of equivalence of some other classes.[54]

For instance, in Russian we distinguish the class of participles P, whose meaning represents the sum of the meanings of the class of verbs V and the class of adjectives A; indeed, its meaning is characterized by all rules of equivalence, which pertain to A, and complemented with the rules which are specific for V (e.g. P can add to itself a verbal object, like V).

If we can describe the meaning of one word class as the sum of the meanings of other word classes, then it is sufficient to distinguish the latter (as the primary ones) for the establishment of the system of word classes in a given language.

D. *The complement of meaning of one class to that of another class (the difference of meanings of the classes)*: $K=F-T$.

Sometimes it is convenient to apply subtraction of meanings of word classes in a language, and to investigate the properties of the difference. It is useful to apply subtraction of meanings in the case of derivative classes.

We can call that word class *derivative*, which is formed from another *initial* class and which includes the rules of equivalence of the initial class so that according to its structure we can partly

[54] In other words, in this case there are two word classes (T and K) in a language such as: (I) each of them is a subclass of a certain third word class (F) of the same language; (II) any rule of equivalence that pertains to the class F, pertains also either to T or to K (or to both).

predict its ability to combine. Derived from a verb are the classes of participles, verbal adverbs, infinitives, gerunds etc. The meaning of a derivative class can be seen as the union of the meaning of the initial class with certain rules of equivalence[55] (i.e. as the sum, the meaning being known of both the sum and one item). To define the meaning of this complement we can subtract the classes.

In some cases the complement of the initial class to the derivative class coincides as to meaning with some class or other of the same language (i.e. a special class can be distinguished characterized in language by the same rules of equivalence as those of the complement obtained). This case was examined in the example of the participial class P, when $P = V + A$.

In other cases the complement may be equivalent as to meaning to a subclass of some class distinguished in the language (i.e. the complement may be seen as a class of the given language, with certain restrictions imposed on its ability to combine). E.g., in Russian a derivative class of adverbial participles G can be distinguished which has all rules of equivalence of V (the initial class) and, moreover, modifies V. In so far as far as in Russian the class Adv is distinguished, whose meaning is determined by the rules: $AdvV \leftrightarrow V$ and $AdvA \leftrightarrow A$, we can define the meaning of the complement of V to G as a subclass of Adv: namely such an Adv', that $Adv'\ V \leftrightarrow V$, but $Adv'A \leftarrow / \rightarrow A$ (for the adverbial participle in Russian can modify a verb, but not an adjective).

Finally we may conceive of a case when the complement of an initial class to a derivative class corresponds as to meaning neither to a special class nor to a subclass of the given language (i.e. the rules of equivalence, forming the complement, are not included into the rules of equivalence of any class in that language).[56] In such a case a new initial meaning can be distinguished in the language (this meaning does not coincide with the meanings of other classes in the given language and is not a subclass of them).

---

[55] As the meaning of a derivative class is always greater than the meaning of an initial class.

[56] This means that a derivative class acquires an entirely new function which is different from the functions of other classes distinguished in the language

It is convenient for some reasons to operate not with the word classes themselves, but with the meanings of word classes which are distinguished in a language. For simplicity's sake we will assume every meaning to have a corresponding word class, which can be distinguished in a language directly (see 0.5.1.) or indireclty (through derivative classes).

Then the system of word classes in a language can be described on the level only of the initial classes, defining the derivative classes through the initial classes.[57]

6.2.1. Having identified the word classes whose meanings coincide, we can describe the system of word classes in one language on various levels.

1) On the level of the initial classes (when only the initial classes are described and their ability to combine with each other (the meanings of the derivative classes can be additionally described through the initial classes)) and on the level of the derivative classes (when all classes are described that are directly distinguished in a language, without distinction as to initial or derivative).

It has been indicated above that these two levels are isomorphous.

2) On the level of classes (when only classes, not subclasses, are distinguished (the latter are obtained supplementarily, by imposing restricting rules)) and on the level of subclasses (i.e. all word classes are described without a division into classes or subclasses). The level of classes is more general, the level of subclasses more particular (the description is more detailed in the last case).[58]

An indispensable condition of typological comparison of word classes in various languages must be the description of the system of word classes inside every language according to the uniform

[57] The description of a system of word classes on the level of initial classes only, is isomorphous to a description on the level of all classes (initial and derivative), because if a certain class can combine with a derivative class, it can definitely combine with the corresponding initial class (on the level of initial classes).

[58] In order to illustrate our points we will describe the system of word classes of Russian. In Russian we find initial classes : N, V, A, Adv; initial subclasses N', A' (pronouns and numerals), Adv' (an Adv that modifies only V, not A); derivative classes: participles $P = A + V$, adverbial participles $G = A + Adv'$, infinitives $I = V + N$.

principles, i.e. on the same level. It is expedient to compare the languages on the more general level.

We shall further investigate and compare the systems of word classes in various languages on the level of initial classes.[59]

7. *The Principles of Identification of Word Classes in Different Languages*

7.1.   With the methods described we can distinguish word classes in a given language and define their relations, i.e. establish the system of word classes. The next step is to compare the systems of word classes in different languages, indentify definite word classes and designate them with the same symbols (e.g. with the symbols *A*, *N*, *V*, *Adv*. etc.); further, word classes of the same designation which belong to different languages can be compared. This can be done by working out a special étalon language; a comparison with this language would allow to determine the meanings of the word classes.

The possibility to work out such an étalon language appears from the following discussion. If the combination of two classes Z and Y in a language is equivalent to $Y(ZY \leftrightarrow Y)$, we can describe these classes through their interrelations. In exactly the same way we can also define other classes inside a given language (in so far as all classes in a language are interrelated); thus, we obtain a chain of correlations. Consequently we can define the classes of every language through each other. It is then sufficient if we can identify one particular class in various languages, in order to define all the remaining classes by it. This enables us to establish a typology of word classes in the form of a calculus.

For instance, having identified a certain class K, we can distinguish in various languages the class (or classes), which modify(s) K, and the class which is modified by K, etc. Thus we can establish a

hierarchy of classes.[60] Accordingly these classes can be designated
by the same symbols in such a way that similarly designated classes
would have one functional meaning. It is reasonable in this
designation to take into account certain typologically predictable
relations of word classes — in other words, our intuitive notion of
the interrelations of various word classes in a language which has a
definite typological value. For instance such relations of word
classes as $AN \longleftrightarrow N$, $VN \longleftrightarrow V$, $AdvV \longleftrightarrow V$, are known to us from our
typological experience, i.e. we know it is usual for A to modify N,
for Adv to modify V, etc. We can assume that these relations take
place in all languages in which the respective word classes are
present. In this case we can designate certain classes in a language
(in particular in an unknown language) as A, N, V, Adv, if their
combinability does not run counter the given relations. Then such
relations, consequently determined and taken as a whole, form a
metalanguage for the determination of the meanings of word classes
in various languages. Ideally (provided this metalanguage is fully
and adequatly formulated) it would be possible to determine the
meaning of any word class in a certain language by comparing it
with a certain other language (through the metalanguage).

7.1.1. Let us illustrate the possibility of designating word classes
in a language (through the identification of their functions) on the
basis of some typologically predictable relations of equivalence.

Let us assume the following: if there are different word classes in a
language, we find the classes N and V in their number.

It is obvious that in this case minimally two word classes can be
differentiated in a language, because if a language contains only one
class, it means that in that language word classes do not differ.

From our assumption follows that if there are only two classes in
a language, these classes are N and V (we are obliged to designate

---

[60]   We note that if a class L modifies in a language a class M, this does not mean
that M cannot modify L (the classes may close the circuit by modifying classes
which define themselves). In the opposite case we would be able to develop a
typology of classes (and establish their taxonomy), having a priori established
the rules of equivalence.

them in that way). Then we may recognize the function of each class, applying the relation: $VN \longleftrightarrow V$.[61]

In a similar way we can also recognize the functions of other word classes. Suppose, there exists in the language a word class Y, different from N and V,[62] such as $XN \longleftrightarrow N$; then we identify X with A (on the basis of comparison with the formula $AN \longleftrightarrow N$). If there is also a class Y, different from N, V and A, and $YV \longleftrightarrow V$, we identify Y with Adv (on the basis of comparison with the formula $AdvV \longleftrightarrow V$). In principle we can assume that in the language a certain class Z can also be distinguished, different from N, V, A, Adv, such a class that $ZA \longleftrightarrow A$.[63] In the same way we can also *a priori* distinguish other classes. At the same time, if a given word class is not specially distinguished in the language in question, its function can be expressed by some of the classes that are present in this language (for instance, if Adv cannot be distinguished, A can express its function: $AV \longleftrightarrow V$). Thus we can determine the function of the word classes and designate them accordingly (substituting the given formulae in the relations of equivalence of the word classes in the language under examination). (These formulae can be regarded as distinctive features of the meanings of respective word classes; indeed, the list of the rules of equivalence, which characterize the meaning of a given word class must contain such rules in which it is possible to substitute the formulae pertaining to that class.)[64]

Thus it is true for all languages in which the respective word

---

[61]   This formula means that the combination of a verb with an object (in an ergative construction — with a subject) is equivalent to a verb.

[62]   If X does not differ from N or V, this means that X can always be substituted for N or V in that language, without disturbing the grammaticalness of the sentence.

[63]   We could not find a language, where such a class could be distinguished, though in principle the existence of such a class is possible.

[64]   It follows that it is sufficient to identify some one word class in a language, in order to recognize all the other word classes according to their ability to combine with this class. It is sometimes proposed that extra-grammatical criteria should be applied to identify this key class: thus, it has been suggested to identify class N as a word class equivalent to a group of proper names which is semantically distinguished in language (cf. the works of K. Ajdukiewicz, I. Bar-Hillel, J. Lambeck *et al.*). It should be mentioned, however that by

classes exist, that $AN \leftrightarrow N$, $VN \leftrightarrow V$, $AdvV \leftrightarrow V$, etc. (because we proceed from these formulae when we ascribe the functions A, N, V, Adv to a class X). In that case a language which would be most desirable as the metalanguage must be the language with the greatest number of possible word classes; indeed, such a language has all the rules of equivalence which characterize any other language.

At the same time we can derive from such an étalon language the different systems of word classes that are typologically possible, by describing the transformations of the change from a language with a greater number of classes to a language with a smaller number of classes. In this way we can obtain a universal typological scheme (a calculus of word classes). On the basis of a comparison with this scheme we can describe the meaning of any word class in an unknown language.[65]

7.1.2. In the described approach the functional distinctions of identically designated word classes in different languages are conditioned by the difference in the number of word classes in

---

carrying the discussion beyond the scope of formal grammatical theory a situation can be created which will adversely affect the results of the interpretation of a typological scheme: for example, it is principally not excluded that the group of proper names will prove to be equivalent in some language to several word class formally distinguished in that language (say, N and A or N and V).

[65] It follows, that the determination of the meanings of word classes in a given language is carried out by successively postulating tentative hypotheses and their consecutive verification by means of the formulae of a metalanguage. The word classes of a language under examination are arbitrarily designated as K, L, M ... (X always designating the class of roots). After that, the relations of equivalence of these classes (determining their combinability) are described, i.e. the system of word classes of the language is established. Then the established system is consecutively compared with all typologically possible systems of word classes, the identification of the word classes thus being achieved: the variables K, L, M ... are successively checked against the values of A, N, V, Adv., until the equivalence rules of our language optimally match the formulae (*resp*. equivalence rules) of the metalanguage.

[It should be noted here that X (designating the class of roots) is a free variable: it can take on any missing value which is sufficient for the designated word class to completely fit into a certain word class of the metalanguage (the function of the root class can be thus compared with that of the joker in card playing).]

these languages (what in some languages is expressed by word
order, acquires a special mode of expression in others). For instance, in amorphous languages word classes are not distinguished
at all; the rules of equivalence are reduced to the only possible:
$XX \leftrightarrow X$. In more complex languages there is a specification and
discernment of the functions (in the sequence from simple to complex, cf. 4.4.); word classes are distinguished and differentiated
accordingly. If in a language two word classes can be distinguished,
we designate them N and V (according to the assumption mentioned
above). This case is typical of the incorporating languages, where
all other functions are usually expressed by mere juxtaposition of
roots (as in amorphous languages). In more complex languages
other functions also find their expression. The more word classes
there are in a language, the more the possibilities of different
combinations, i.e. the more different rules of equivalence characterizing the word classes.

Thus a word class in one language can correspond as to its
function to several classes in another, more complex language. In
general, the main idea of the suggested approach is to define word
classes not by intralinguistic methods but through correspondence
with other languages (at the same time intralinguistic methods
are applied when distinguishing between the word classes within a
language); these correspondences are established by means of a
metalanguage. Thus we avoid the contradictions that can arise if
we do not consider interlinguistic relations. For instance, the verb
in Paleosiberian languages corresponds as to its functions both to
verb and adjective in other languages (with a greater number of
classes);[66] the same in Korean.[67] The noun in Amharic or Arabic
corresponds both to noun and adjective of other languages,[68]
etc. Such a comparison obviously presupposes an étalon language.

[66] *See* R. Jakobson, "Langues paléo-sibériennes", *Les Languges du monde*,
(Paris, 1952), p. 417; also *Jazyki i pis'mennost' narodov Severa* [Languages and
Writings of Peoples of the North] (Moscow-Leningrad, 1934) pp. 165, 183.
[67] *See* G. Ramstedt, *Grammatika korejskogo jazyka* [Grammar of the Korean
language] (Moscow, 1951) p. 85).
[68] *See* N. V. Jušmanov, *Amxarskij jazyk* [Amharic]. (Moscow, 1959), p. 23.

7.2. We can choose or establish a complex étalon language (metalanguage) with a maximum number of classes; it will have the most widely differing rules of equivalence. Then, by means of correspondence with this metalanguage, we can describe the meanings of the word classes in various languages. Any other language will be, by definition, simpler than the metalanguage (on account of the number of word classes) — some two word classes of the metalanguage will coincide in this language, i.e. a certain word class in a language, less complex than the metalanguage, will cover the meaning of two or more classes of the metalanguage. A word class, that covers the meaning of several classes of the metalanguage (or in general — of a more complex language possessing a larger number of word classes), can be conceived as the result of the neutralization of these classes; we can tentatively do away with the formal distinctions between different word classes of the metalanguage and thus, consecutively diminishing the number of classes, investigate the modifications ensuing in the rules of equivalence.

Thus altering the metalanguage (i.e. consecutively identifying some two classes and substituting the significations of one class in the rules of equivalence characterizing another class) we must obtain a universal pattern, which corresponds with any of the languages under examination.

7.2.1. Suppose a relatively complex metalanguage with classes A, V, N, Adv.

Let us describe the rules of equivalence for that language:[69]

$$AN \longleftrightarrow N$$
$$NN \longleftrightarrow N$$
$$VN \longleftrightarrow V^{70}$$
$$NV \longleftrightarrow V^{71}$$

---

[69] In the formulae the attribute precedes the attributed, the object follows the verb. Thus we distinguish between complementation and attribution (for attempt to define attributive and completive types of relation in terms of transformation, see B. A. Uspensky, "Opyt transformacionnogo issledovanija sintaksičeskoj tipologii" [An attempt to transformational investigation of syntactic typology] Issledovanija po strukturnoj tipologii, Moscow, 1963.

[70] Object of V.

[71] Attribute of V.

$$AdvV\longleftrightarrow V$$
$$NA\longleftrightarrow A$$
$$AdvA\longleftrightarrow A$$

The Russian language, for example belongs to this type.[72]

Let us now imagine a simpler language, where classes Adv and A are not formally differentiated; by substituting A for Adv in the above language we obtain classes A, N, V.

The rules are:

$$AN\longleftrightarrow N$$
$$NN\longleftrightarrow N$$
$$VN\longleftrightarrow V$$
$$NV\longleftrightarrow V$$
$$AV\longleftrightarrow V$$
$$NA\longleftrightarrow A$$
$$AA\longleftrightarrow A\text{[73]}$$

The Danish language belongs to this type.

Imagine an even simpler language where classes A and N are not formally differentiated; by substituting N for A in the above language we obtain classes N and V.

The rules are:

$$NN\longleftrightarrow N$$
$$VN\longleftrightarrow V$$
$$NV\longleftrightarrow V$$

The Arabic language belongs to this type.

Imagine a language with the same number of classes, where A and V are not formally differentiated; by substituting V for A in the last but one language (with classes N, V, A) we obtain the same classes N, V, characterized however by other rules of equivalence.

---

[72] In order to illustrate some unobvious combinations we shall draw some examples from Russian: NN — "izba lesnika, nožka ot stula" [the hut of the forester, the leg of the chair]; NA — "krasivyj licom, smelyj v boju" [beautiful as regard the face, bold in the battle).

[73] This formula is redundant; it may be obtained from the preceding formulae.

The rules are:

$$VN \longleftrightarrow N$$
$$NN \longleftrightarrow N$$
$$VN \longleftrightarrow V^{74}$$
$$NV \longleftrightarrow V$$
$$VV \longleftrightarrow V$$

The Guilyak language belongs to this type.

When further decreasing the number of classes, we obtain only one class: $V=N=X$,

and one rule:

$$XX \longleftrightarrow X$$

The amorphous languages belong to this type.

7.2.2.   We note that the suggested procedure of identifications (i.e. identifying in the sequence $Adv \to A \langle{}^{N}_{V})$ is sufficient to define any system of word classes, if their number is not more than 4. It is easy to check (arbitrarily identifying any two classes of our metalanguage) that in any other identification the system obtained can be in general reduced to one of the systems already obtained. Accordingly we may establish a hierarchy of word classes (for all languages that have word classes):

$$N, V$$
$$A$$
$$Adv$$

and we can postulate, that the identifications may only be effected upwards and in consecutive order (without missing a stage).

In the same way we can develop a metalanguage with a maximum number of classes; by comparison with this metalanguage we would be able to describe the meanings of the word classes of any language.

[74]   Here we meet with a contradiction: VN is equivalent both to N and V (i.e. it may be both an object to a verb and an attribute to a noun). In a real language, apparently, supplementary indications will exist on a more concrete level allowing to differentiate between these constructions (say, through the case of the noun or the form of the verb).

But even if we do not develop a universal metalanguage, we may describe the meaning of a class of one language through its correspondence with another language. For instance, the Arabic N corresponds with the Russian N, A and Adv; the Gilyak V covers the meanings of the Russian A, Adv and V. Accordingly their meanings may be regarded as the logical sums of the meanings of the word classes in Russian: Arabic $N =$ Russian $(N+A+Adv)$; Gilyak $V =$ Russian $(V+A+Adv)$. In this case the Russian as a more complex language plays the part of the metalanguage (inside this restricted scope of languages).

The suggested approach demonstrates the possibility to set up a metalanguage for the characterization of the meanings of the classes in various languages, as well as to apply formal procedures to the meanings of various word classes in order to obtain different *a priori* systems (with a view of establishing correlations between these systems and actual natural languages).

We may note that, when comparing word classes, we use, apart from a special étalon language also an amorphous étalon language. Therefore the special (complex) étalon language for the determination of the meanings of word classes can be regarded as supplementary.

8. *Some Concluding Statements*

8.1. In the structure of an amorphous metalanguage various possibilities have merged syncretically according to which a language can become complex. Thus, the structure $XXXX...$ in combination with bracket-elements[75] is characterized by the absence of indispensable categories and by the homogeneity of the classes. Accordingly a language can become more complex by the introduction, distribution and synthetical expression of indispensable categories as well as by the increase of the number of classes. Both of these indices are essential for the characterization of a language: for instance, in Arabic only classes N and V are distinguished, but

[75] Bracket-elements are elements II2 indicating the sequence of contraction, indispensable, as has been indicated (3.1.2), for an amorphous language.

the language is more complex than two-classes languages usually are; at the same time German knows relatively many classes; but nevertheless unformed root elements can also exist in this language; the same is the case in Chukot.[76] We therefore propose to appraise the complexity of languages (not of constructions) — and to classify them accordingly — on the basis of comparison with an amorphous étalon-language by two parameters: 1) the number of transformations when changing from the given structure to an amorphous structure; 2) the number of transformations with regard to the identification of the word classes when changing from the given language to an amorphous language (we find that the number of these transformations corresponds with the number of word classes in the given language).

These two bases of comparison are regarded as the most essential (in so far as both the syntagmatics and paradigmatics of a language are thus characterized); at the same time we may also use other bases for comparison.

8.2. The more complex a language is, the more functions will be formally differentiated in it (i.e. the more classes there will be); at the same time the more numerous restrictions will be imposed on its structure.

In an amorphous language any combination of root elements is grammatical. With the growth of the complexity of a language, the number of structural combinations prohibited (i.e. of grammatically incorrect combinations) in that language increases.

In drawing a table of correspondences for the structures of various languages from simple to complex we can change from one structure to another, using the prohibited structural combinations and replacing them by corresponding correct combinations (in

---

[76] In Chukot the same elements can incorporate, or else they get special grammatical modification and form an agglutinative structure (*see* P. J. Skorik, "Inkorporacija v čukotskom jazyke kak sposob vyraženija sintaksičeskix otnošenij" [Incorporation in Chukot as a means to express syntactic relations], *Izvestija otdelenija literatury i jazyka Akademii Nauk SSSR*, VI (1947), 6.

practice this means the use, for instance, of broken Russian when changing from Russian to another language).[77]

All relations in an amorphous language are of uniform type but if we increase the complexity of a language, the relations between its units become differentiated. Thus, in respect to amorphous languages there is no point in defining the function of a given structural sequence, i.e. in investigating whether it is contractable to one class or to such sequence of classes that cannot be further contracted to any of its part (in the latter case the structural sequence under investigation corresponds with a sentence, whereas in the former case if corresponds with a certain part of a sentence). In other words, in an amorphous language predicative, attributive,[78] or completive,[79] etc. combinations are not distinguished (e.g. the

[77] Such a table may be useful for translation. For instance, in the table of correspondences from English to Russian we will find:

N_2	N_1	→	A	N
delo	čelovek		delovoj	čelovek
business man				

i.e. an indication to look for such an A $(delovoj,)$ that would correspond with the Russian N_2 $(delo)$.

[78] Analogically in other languages: Aleutian [see V. I. Ioxel'son, *Unanganskij (aleutskij) jazyk* [Unangian (Aleutian) jazyki] *Jazyki i pis'mennost' narodov Severa*, III, Moscow-Leningrad, 1934) p. 142; Yurak (*see* I. I. Meščaninov, "Ergativnyj stroj" [The ergative system], *Jazyk i myslenie*, XI, 1948, p. 236 and others). This phenomenon is also reflected in a series of languages, where the same elements designate an attributive relation being combined with a noun but a completive or a predicative relation when combined with a verb. Nearly all forms of the Arabic suffixed pronouns belong to this type, as well as some forms of the Tajik and Turkish personal inflections.

All these phenomena may be appraised as relatively close to the structure of a metalanguage.

We must, apparently, similarly appraise cases of identical grammatical form of noun and verb, which is characteristic for Aranta (*see* A. Sommerfelt, *La Langue et la Société* (Oslo, 1938), pp. 73, 109, 189), for Gilyak (*see* E. A. Krejnovič, "Ob inkorporaci v nivxskom jazyke" [On incorporation in Gilyak], *Voprosy jazykoznanija*, 1958, 6, p. 29.

[79] N. F. Jakovlev distinguishes in Adyge a special type of grammatically unformed "attributive objects"; it is supposed, that they "represent that general part of sentence in which attribute and object were not yet discriminated (differentiated) from each other ... In most cases they can be understood in two ways: as an indefinite attribute and as an object".

Chinese *njao fej* means both "the bird flies"[80] and "bird flight");
when increasing the complexity of a language these differences
emerge.

A language can be regarded as a certain structure plus the rules
which transform this structure into concrete sentences; the method
of metalanguage enables us to divide that structure into the
fundamental structure (the structure of the metalanguage) plus
the rules which transform it into the structure of the given structural
class of languages. In this sense setting up a typology with respect
to a certain étalon-language can be regarded as a possible approach
to a universal grammar.

Appendix to the Classification of Formative Elements[81]

Tajik
/ *Dar* / *osmon/i* / *sof/i* / *begubor* / *sitora* / *x,o* / *me/duraxš/id/and/*
"In the pure, clear sky stars were twinkling"

dar Xi Xi X Xx,o meX id and

dar-	preposition	II2
-i	exponent of *izafet*	II1
x,x,o	exponent of plural	II1
me-	exponent of continuative	II1
-id	exponent of past tense	II1
-and	exponent of 3rd p.pl.	II1

Turkish
/ *Mukadderat/ın/a* / *iştirak* / *et/mek/le* / *gurur* / *duy/makta/yız* /
"We feel proud, because we take part in his fate"

[80] *Njao* — "bird, birds", *fej* — "flight, to fly"; here it is necessary to consider,
that a specification of tense, expressed in the English "flies" is absent in the
corresponding amorphous structure.
[81] The appendix is constructed in the following way: we list: a) the name of
the language; b) a sentence in that language, divided by vertical lines into
elements (if linear segmentation is possible); c) translation of the sentence into
English; d) the structure of the sentence, where the root elements are designated
as *X*, the formative elements being given in their actual form; e) characterization
of the formative elements as II1 and II2; in some cases the basis for the characterization of the elements is also indicated.

Xına X Xmekle X X maktayiz

-ın	possessive suffix of 3rd p.sg.	II2
-a	exponent of dative	II2
-mek	exponent of infinitive	III1
-le	exponent of sociative	II2
-makta	exponent of duration	III1
-yiz	exponent of 1st p.pl.	III1

German

| *Die* | *Zahl* | *der* | *neue/n* | *Wohn/häus/er* | *in* | *unser/er* | *Vor/stadt* | *beläuf/t* | *sich* | *auf* | *einig/e* | *hundert* |

"The number of new dwelling houses in our suburb runs to several hundreds"

die X der Xn XXer in Xer X XXt X auf Xe X

die, der-	articles	II2
-n	exponent of plural	III1
-er	exponent of plural	III1
in-	preposition	II2
-er	exponent of case	III1
-t	exponent of 3rd p.sg.	III1
auf-	preposition	II2
-e	exponent of number	III1

Russian

| *Mašin/a* | *vy/exa/l/a* | *iz* | *les/a* |

"The car drove out of the wood"

Xa vyXala iz Xa

-a	exponent of fem., sg., nom.	III1
vy-	exponent of perfect aspect	III1
-al	exponent of noun	III1
iz-	preposition; governs gen.case	II2
-a	exponent of genitive case	III1

Chukot

| *Čavčyva/ta kora/t* | *ny/pela/kenat* |

"Raindeer-breeders leave the raindeer"

Xta Xt nyXkenat

-ta	exponent of ergative case	II2
-t	exponent of absolute case	II2
ny-kenat	exponent of 3rd p.pl.IInd pr.tense	II2[82]

Esperanto

| La |čef|a|j | urb|a|j | gazet|o|j informs|is | pri | la | vizit|o | de | la | pol|a | delegaci|o |

"The main city newspapers gave information of the visit of the Polish delegation"

la Xaj Xaj Xoj Xis pri la Xo de la Xa Xo

la-	article	II2
-a-	exponent of adjective	III1
-o-	exponent of noun	III1
-j-	exponent of plural	III1
-is	exponent of finite form in past tense	III1
pri	preposition	II2
de-	preposition	II2

Aranta[83]

| Atua | na|la | ara|na | erku|ka |

"This man seized a kangaroo"

X Xla Xna Xka

-la	exponent of activity;	II2
	here: exponent of ergat. case	
	Defines the group	
	atua na (this man); without attribute	
	it would have been *atuala*	
-na	exponent of direction (allative case)	II2
	Cf. *ara ntjarana* ("many kangaroo's")	
-ka	exponent of past tense	II2
	(here) and also of genitive case	
	Cf. *wotta erkuka* (again seized)	

---

[82] We may say, changing the construction into an intransitive one and therefore changing the ergative case into an absolute case:

Čavčyvat nykorapelakenat

Xt   nyXXkenat

(the meaning is the same).

[83] A characterization of the formative elements in Aranta is to a certain extent hypothetical; therefore the basis for the given characterization is given.

Arabic

Yakūnu-rriğālu kamā turīdu-nnisā'u[84]

"Men are such, as the women want"

| *X* | vocalism of imperfect of the I rootpattern / confix 3rd p. sg. masc. / *al* / *X* / vocalism pluralis fractus / *ka* / *X* / *X* / vocalism of imperfect of the IV rootpattern / confix 3rd p. sg. fem. / *al* / *X* / vocalism pluralis fractus /

vocalism of imperfect		II1
y - u	confix 3rd p.sg.masc.	II1
al-	article	II1
ka-	preposition	II2
vocalism of imperfect of the IV rootpattern		II1
t - u	confix 3rd p. sg.fem.	II1
vocalism pluralis fractus		II1

---

[84]   A direct segmentation in the sentence is impossible; it is shown linearly.